GENE SARAZEN AND
SHELL'S WONDERFUL WORLD OF GOLF

GENE SARAZEN AND *SHELL'S WONDERFUL WORLD OF GOLF*

By Al Barkow

With Mary Ann Sarazen

Foreword by Byron Nelson

Clock Tower Press, LLC
3622 W. Liberty
Ann Arbor, MI 48103
www.clocktowerpress.com

Printed and bound in Canada.

10 9 8 7 6 5 4 3 2 1

Library of Congress Cataloging-in-Publication Data

Barkow, Al.
    Gene Sarazen and Shell's wonderful world of golf / by Al Barkow with Mary Ann Sarazen ; foreword by Byron Nelson.
        p. cm.
    ISBN 1-932202-05-6
    1. Sarazen, Gene. 2. Shell's wonderful world of golf (Television program) 3. Television broadcasting of sports—United States. 4. Golf—United States—History. I. Title: Shell's wonderful world of golf. II. Sarazen, Gene. III. Sarazen, Mary Ann. IV. Title.
    GV967.B312 2003
    796.352'092—dc21

                                        2003010871

Photographs from the Gene Sarazen collection, with permission from Shell Oil Company, are utilized throughout the book.

DEDICATION

To the late Fred Raphael, who gave me the chance.

Al Barkow

To my mother and father, Mary and Gene Sarazen.

Mary Ann Sarazen

CONTENTS

FOREWORD

By Byron Nelson

It's always a pleasure to look back on your career and count the times you've been in the vanguard, one of the first to do something different that adds long-term value to your line of work. So it has been the case with the original *Shell's Wonderful World of Golf* television program. Gene Littler and I were chosen to play the first match filmed for the program. Gene was, at the time, in the prime of his career, having just won the U.S. Open Championship. I had been retired from competitive golf for some years by then (1961), and was very pleased that the folks who put the show together thought I still had enough of a game to give young Gene a run for the money.

Just to be sure, I put in some extra time on the practice tee before traveling to New Jersey for the filming. I must say, though, that it wasn't only Gene Littler I was preparing for. The match was being played on the famous Pine Valley Golf Club course, one of the toughest in the game then, just as it is to this day.

As it happened, neither Gene nor I were ready for the time it took in between shots for the cameras to be moved and set up. That may have had something to do with our scores, which were not as good as we would have liked them to be. I don't think I was ready, either, for the response the show would get. As is pointed out in this book, the ratings for the show in its first year were a little disappointing by advertising standards, but at least two million people saw the program and were very pleased. So much so that the Shell show eventually gained a quite substantial audience.

That was the overriding value of the show. It gave the game of golf a very attractive exposure—the travelogues alone were worth the price of admission—that went a long way toward promoting the game into what is now a major sport in this country, and the world. Newer generations of golf fans may wonder about that remark in light of the millions of dollars today's golfers play for on the pro tours, but back in 1960 golf was still a game with a relatively small and somewhat elite following. The Shell show helped immensely to change that image, that position in the world of sports. I am very pleased to have been a part of that transformation.

PREFACE

Shell's Wonderful World of Golf wasn't the very first made-for-television golf program, but it might just as well have been. It was second by about two years to "All-Star Golf, " but the Shell show's impact on the popularity of golf, its influence on international travel and resort golf, and on the production values of future televised golf, far outdistanced its predecessor. The geographic scope of the program was, at the time, truly amazing. Whoever thought golf was played in Thailand? Or Greece, for goodness sake? American golfers discovered they could take their clubs along on a trip to the ancient home of western civilization, and after a tour of the Parthenon get in 18 holes. Well now!

The Shell show also reminded those already devoted to golf how splendid a diversion they had. It reinforced their engagement with the game. How could golfers, however much feeling they already had for their game, not be enchanted anew when on the relatively new and still astounding medium—television—they were brought pictures of beautiful courses in the majestic Canadian Rockies, on the islands of Bermuda, Jamaica, and Eleuthera, wherever that was; or just around the corner from the Vatican—yes, *the* Vatican. What's more, playing on those courses were the best golfers of the time, and in some cases of all time—from Nelson, Hogan, and Snead, to Palmer, Player, and Nicklaus, not to mention outstanding foreign players who had hitherto been only names (and grainy black-and-white pictures) in the newspapers—Roberto DeVicenzo, Peter Thomson, Henry Cotton, Flory Van Donck.

All of this surely stimulated lightweight golfers to put more meat on their commitment to the game. And while there are no numbers to support the claim, the Shell show surely motivated many thousands, maybe even millions who had never played before to take up the old Scots game.

On a more subjective level, the Shell Show was a significant, life-altering adventure for those who were closest to it. It gave its original producer, and director for the last five years, Fred Raphael, a career he never dreamed of while growing up in a tenement district of Jersey City, New Jersey. Out of Raphael's involvement with the Shell show came his notion of a tournament for retired professional golfers, The Legends of Golf. That program's popularity led directly to the founding of the Senior PGA Tour. And so it can be said that a breakthrough concept devised for television in the 1960s carried over into the twenty-first century and affected the playing careers, indeed the lives, of hundreds of middle-aged and older professional golfers.

The Shell show most certainly renewed, extended, and expanded the golf life of Gene Sarazen, to whom this book is dedicated. For all his wonderful accomplishments as a champion golfer, by 1960, when the Shell show was only an idea in its germination stage, Sarazen was a ghost of the sporting world's past. It had been 20 years since he last appeared in a serious golf tournament. Albeit it was quite an appearance. He reached a play-off for the 1940 U.S. Open, which he lost to Lawson Little. Still, to a nation whose historical perspective tended to reach back only as far as the scores of the yesterday's ball games, his was only a name in the record books that few ever looked into. Sarazen felt this himself, as do all sports heroes of past eras. It didn't trouble him. He was busy working in public relations, tending to his farm in Germantown, New York, being a devoted husband to his wife, Mary, and a father to his two children, Mary Ann and Gene Jr., and grandfather to their children. Still, he had once been the talk of the sports world, one of the great players of his or any other era, someone who was welcomed into the company of royalty, the nabobs of big business, and the brightest stars of the entertainment world. That was heady stuff, hard to forget. So, when the opportunity to be the host of a television golf program became a reality, Sarazen recognized immediately that it was (or could be) a rebirth of the career that meant the most to him. It proposed a return to the game that had transformed his life in the first place. He had a moment of doubt at the very beginning, when the call first came, but not long after, he wrote in one of the many letters to his good friend Bobby Jones that getting the job was "my greatest break."

There were other golfers or golf persons of note who might have been anointed the host of *Shell's Wonderful World of Golf.* Some were considered. For example, Tommy Armour, who had a dramatic silver-haired presence and the vocal delivery of a stage actor. Henry Longhurst, the mustachioed British golf writer who at the time was famously understating television coverage of play at the 16th hole of the Masters tournament, was a possible choice. Byron Nelson could also have fit the bill. He already had experience as a commentator on televised golf programs, and his name was closer to the top of the general public's memory bank. His remarkable 11-tournament winning streak was only 15 years old, and he did not entirely quit competing in big-time golf until the mid-1950s. But Herbert Warren Wind, the preeminent golf writer/historian of his time, and the first writer on the Shell show, recommended Sarazen. Those who made the final decisions saw this as the right call. Sarazen had won all four of the modern major championships (U.S. and British Opens, the U.S. PGA and the Masters tournament), and was in fact the first to achieve this quadfecta. Only Ben Hogan had matched it, up to then. Sarazen had holed that fantastic 4-wood for a double-eagle in the 1935 Masters, and in his association with Walter Hagen, had harked back to the rise of American dominance in golf. Furthermore, he dressed smartly in knickers, a universally recognized sartorial symbol of the game. In all, casting Sarazen had just the right historical/nostalgic tone the program wanted.

Sarazen's contribution to *Shell's Wonderful World of Golf* tilted the American golfers' mind-set to where it had a deeper feeling for the history of the game. Through his appearance every weekend during the winter for nine years, golfers coming into the game in the 1950s and '60s were reminded or instructed that golf was not invented just the other day by the great idol of the moment, Arnold Palmer.

My personal experience with Gene Sarazen was especially memorable, a highlight of my golfing life. As the golf writer (and eventually an associate producer) of the show, I traveled with the production crew to all the locations. One of my charges was to write Gene's opening monologue, in which he described the course on which the match was being played. We usually arrived about three days before the match was to be filmed, which gave us plenty of time to play the course, learn about it, and find ways to describe it. Gene and I played often together for this "research."

I was in my early 30s, and had kept up my game. Only four years earlier, in 1959, I played number two man on a NAIA (National Association of Intercollegiate Athletics) national championship golf team (for Western Illinois University). Gene was in his early 60s, and quite strong and agile. He was, indeed, a physical phenomenon. He withstood the rigors of world travel from his 20s right into his 90s, when he continued to take a good swing at the ball as an honorary starter at the Masters tournament. We had excellent games. There was no money on them. Gene would have none of that. In his matter-of-fact way he cited the economic reality that I was a mere writer (which is to say, not well funded) and he was a man of considerable means. It didn't have to be about money. We played our hearts out every time for the sheer joy of competition. It was some of the most intensely competitive golf I've ever played.

The crowning moment came at Turnberry, the wonderful links on the west coast of Scotland. We stayed in the massive, imposing British Railway Hotel at the top of the hill overlooking Turnberry's two courses (and the Ailsa Craig, an immense stone rising out of the Irish Sea that seemed always cast in a mystic mist). We had breakfast under the chandeliers in the elegant dining room, its tables thick with padding, the silver heavy and ornate, the waiters in formal clothing.

Kippers, eggs, sausage, tea, toast. Then we both shoed up and walked down the long concrete stairway from the hotel right onto the Ailsa course. We had no trouble getting a starting time, not only because it was Gene Sarazen wanting to play, but also because in those days resort golf travel was not what it would become after the Shell series had its run. In a word, there was hardly a soul on the course. It just doesn't get any better than that.

The last time around Turnberry for us was the day before we were to begin filming the match between Dave Marr and Dave Thomas. I was much taken by the Ailsa course, which is not surprising. It is one of the finest true links courses in the world. We played 18 holes on a brisk but sunny day, and this being the last chance at the course I wanted to get one more shot at the fabulous ninth hole. It plays from a tee perched high on a promontory overlooking an ever-boiling sea crashing onto the side of the steep sea wall. The direct line to the hole requires a drive that must carry some 210 yards over an inlet of the sea. Not a long carry by ordinary standards, but almost invariably into a strong wind. It's a daunting tee-shot, a wonderful challenge. I asked Gene if he would play another nine, so we could play the hole again. There were no carts on which we could ride out to the ninth hole, and I suppose we could have taken a couple of clubs and walked out to the hole itself. But we didn't. We played out to it. At first, Sarazen said he was not that anxious to play all the way out there again. But as I came to realize, he had a way of initially rejecting proposals then coming to enjoy them when he took them up. I like to believe I talked him into the extra nine, but I don't think it took all that much. He loved playing golf, and while he might not have said so, he also had a thing for that tee-shot at the ninth.

We played through eight holes, and now were looking at an even more intimidating than usual drive. The wind had increased in velocity. The sea was at full boil, the waves pounding loudly just beneath us. The carry over the inlet was truly heroic. I hit first, and while I (swear) meant to try to clear the inlet, I ended up bailing out to the right. Not Gene. With great resolve, undoubtedly the same sort he had when he won all his championships, Sarazen took his compact but forceful swing and drilled his drive dead over the inlet and on line with the stone marker denoting the center of the fairway. Of course he carried the water, but it was the margin that was impressive. It was a terrific display. He said not a word about that drive, or showed in any obvious way how pleased he was with it. That was not the way of athletes from of his era. No one hotdogged it then—no animated jigs, fist pumps, shouts of exaltation. But when I glanced back at him immediately after his ball cleared the inlet, I saw a flicker of pride and pleasure on his face. Carrying that great wide gash in the landscape meant nothing to the record books, but that was beside the point. He did it, and in his doing it I experienced, by indirection, something of what it was to be a truly great golfer.

I must say that on the shows themselves, the audience did not get to hear the Gene Sarazen everyone on the production staff knew. Somehow, in doing his opening monologue and even when giving the color commentary of the match as it progressed, his true character did not come through. Off camera he was an excellent storyteller, with a fine if somewhat acerbic sense of humor. He was articulate, and especially insightful about human nature. And by all means, he knew his golf, the nature of the game, and those who play it. He became somewhat looser when Jimmy Demaret came on as cohost and play-by-play announcer, but even then he was not the Sarazen we enjoyed at dinner or at the bar of an evening when he was having a glass of Old Rarity, the scotch whiskey he prized. It's hard to imagine that a man who played before thousands of people at a time for years on end, and gave innumerable award-acceptance speeches, would more or less freeze in front of a camera. But, as the saying goes, talking for a living is hard to do. Then again, the fact that he didn't come off as a smooth-talking, slick wordsmith was what made Sarazen's contribution to the show so poignant and effective. His homelier on-camera style made him more believable.

In any case, there was never any thought of replacing Gene Sarazen as the host of *Shell's Wonderful World of Golf.* He was as permanent a fixture as the show itself became. The show had a nine-year run, in which 92 matches were played, in 48 countries. The show touched down on every continent on earth. It was a remarkably long life for a television series, particularly one aimed at a relatively small corner of the population. The story of how that came to be is what this book is about. Pictures accompany it from Gene Sarazen's personal collection, which are part of the Gene and Mary Sarazen Foundation that is under the direction of his daughter, Mary Ann. She has put together an introduction to this volume which gives us another perspective on the show and her father's association with it.

ACKNOWLEDGMENTS

Our thanks to the following for their recall of events that are part of this history. They include Hal Power, who was a fountain of information; Byron Nelson, Jack Burke Jr., Dick Darley, Edna Forde, Charlie Okun, and Dick Ashe. Also, the Bob Jones family for allowing us the use of the Bob Jones–Gene Sarazen correspondence. And Chris Normyle of the Shell Company for the generous use of photographs and the show's name.

Al Barkow & Mary Ann Sarazen

INTRODUCTION

Little did anyone realize how continuous the popularity of *Shell's Wonderful World of Golf* would be, least of all my dad. I remember so well the excitement that was generated in the family when Herb Wind called to offer Dad a chance to be the host of the program, and all the more when he got the job. Dad didn't realize how long that commitment would last, or the wonderful opportunities it meant for him, and for golf. It came to him over time. Years after the show ended, as Dad traveled to receive honors in Japan, England, Ireland, and in the United States, mention of the Shell show was always a part of the introductions. People remembered him from those shows almost as much as for his wonderful playing career, and when the show was mentioned it would be interesting to hear Dad add to it by way of anecdotes. He would talk at length about the beautiful areas of the world he had visited, and the interesting people, including a few kings, queens, and princesses, he and Mother met.

Of all the shows he worked on, the one in Atlanta was always Dad's favorite because in it he interviewed—had a nice chat, actually—with Bob Jones. He had a lifelong warm, special relationship with Bob Jones. They had great respect for each other, and in that interview it was evident. So is it in the letters he wrote regularly to Jones, many of which appear in this book.

During the years the shows were being filmed, my brother, Gene, and I were busy raising our families and did not have much time to travel to locations. However, I was living in the Boston area when the match between Billy Casper and Doug Sanders was being played at The Country Club, and Dad had me come out to the filming. It was great fun to meet everyone on the production staff, make friends with many of them, and see how a television program was made.

Mother, on the other hand, with Gene and I grown, traveled with Dad to many of the locations. She enjoyed very much visiting the local museums, parks, and other special places in parts of the world I don't think she thought, as a young girl or even as a grown woman, she would ever visit. Of course, she also did her share of shopping. But most of her purchases were gifts for her grandchildren, and for my brother and me. My charm bracelet to this day has many charms from foreign lands that she gave me.

Many friendships continued long after the series ended. Gordon Bigger and his wife, Naomi, visited more than a few times the farm in Germantown, New York, and our home in Florida. Herb Wind called and wrote regularly, and Fred Raphael always stayed in touch with Dad. Both Herb and Fred joined us in Florida in 1992, to celebrate Dad's 90th birthday. Fred invited Dad to play in the inaugural Legends of Golf tournament he created in 1978. Indeed, the name of the show came to Fred after a conversation with Dad at a Masters tournament. Dad played in it quite a few times afterward.

We heard always from Hal Power, the Shell public relations officer who traveled with the show. He was also the still photographer on the show, and gave many of the pictures in this book to Dad to be part of his personal collection. Edna Forde kept in touch with Dad over all the years, and in 1993 Dad paid her a visit in Ireland. Long-term bonds were formed between the Sarazen family and many of the people who worked on *Shell's Wonderful World of Golf.*

Even during the last year of Dad's life he was still watching *Shell's Wonderful World of Golf* on the Golf Channel. Which leads one to believe that all these many years after the shows were first aired there is still interest in the program, and the behind-the-scenes story of it. Al Barkow, who traveled with the show as the golf writer and associate producer for six years, had firsthand knowledge of the trials and tribulations, and many fine moments, that were experienced in the filming. He deserves the credit for putting all that together in this book. I thank him for his expertise.

Gene Sarazen
and
Shell's Wonderful World of Golf

AN IDEA GETS A LIFE

◆ ◆ ◆

Golf has been blessed during its long history by the periodic appearance of individuals with influence who supported the game in ways that greatly increased its popularity and growth. Some did it for no other reason than their personal love of the game. Others were in it strictly for business reasons. More often than not it was a combination of these motives that shaped the charitable action of golf's benefactors. For instance, the Duke of Windsor, an avid golfer, showed a streak of royal egalitarianism when he forcefully broke down the long-standing social dictate in Great Britain that kept golf professionals from entering the clubhouses of private clubs. One day in the 1930s, after a round of golf with the outstanding British golf professional Archie Compston, Compston was not allowed to join the Duke in the clubhouse of the Royal Berkshire GC, in England. The prince was incensed and warned the club that if it did not allow Compston to join him that day, and didn't change its rule, it would lose its royal status. The club wasted no time. It allowed Compston entry to its inner sanctum that day, and changed its restrictive rule. In time this act carried over to American private clubs that held the same elitist attitude. The opening gave professionals a greater sense of belonging to the game, and encouraged among them a more enthusiastic participation in its heritage and history.

American presidents, beginning with William Howard Taft and followed by Woodrow Wilson, Warren Harding, and Dwight D. Eisenhower, played a lot of golf while in the highest and most prominent office in the land. The wide publicity their golf acquired in the press spread interest in the game. Taft was the first, and was particularly avid, going so far as to ignore the criticism of former President Theodore Roosevelt, who thought golf was a game for sissies and should not be played by the nation's leader. Another member of the Roosevelt clan who attained the presidency, Franklin D., did not hold so cramped a conviction. He had been an ardent golfer before being stricken with polio and as president encouraged the continuation of the PGA Tour during World War II as a way of easing the burden of America's war-effort workers with its entertainment value.

Numerous show business personalities have broadened the appeal for golf not only by playing the game, but also by financially supporting professional tournaments. Richard Arlen, for instance, a Hollywood star of the 1920s and '30s, put up prize money for the Los Angeles Open when the event was threatened with cancellation during the Great Depression. Bing Crosby was the first show business person to officially sponsor a regular tour event. The Bing Crosby National Pro-Am was begun in 1937, and exists to this day (as the AT&T Pebble Beach National Pro-Am). Because so many of the amateurs in the event were also well-known entertainers, the tournament and golf gained a large audience. Bob Hope followed Crosby's lead, beginning in 1960. With a similar format including not only show business stars but also political luminaries, the Hope has always attracted a substantial television rating. Other singers who were keen golfers got involved in backing professional tournament golf—Perry Como, Andy Williams, Dean Martin, and Glen Campbell. Comedians Danny Thomas and Jackie Gleason, and all-around star Sammy Davis Jr. are other show business luminaries who attached their celebrity to the old Scotsgame.

Many business executives have combined their affection for golf with efforts to use it to enhance their businesses. This has long been the case in American golf, and it has greatly expanded golf's prominence. In the early days of the pro tour, Chambers of Commerce and resort hotels sponsored tournaments as a way to tell the world the virtues of their towns or hostels as places to live, do business, or have a nice vacation. This development grew to encompass major corporate sponsorships of PGA Tour events, which is now the bedrock of the circuit.

Some decisions among corporations to get involved financially in the pro tour or otherwise in golf have been made by committee meetings in boardrooms. But individuals, often flamboyant personalities who made all the decisions, have triggered for the most part corporate involvement. One such was George S. May, the founder and owner of George S. May International, a firm that specializes in bringing failing companies back to good health. May also owned and operated the Tam O'Shanter Country Club in a north suburb of Chicago, and beginning in the 1940s he began sponsoring professional tournaments at his course. He meant to enhance his primary business through the exposure of his eponymous business firm via well-publicized golf events. May made sure they were well publicized by putting up exceptionally high purse money. His story is relevant here because May initiated the first live national network telecast of competitive golf.

For two consecutive weeks in August, beginning in the mid 1940s and continuing through the mid-1950s, May staged the Tam O'Shanter All-American tournaments and the "World" Championships. The program consisted of tournaments for both men and women professionals and amateurs—four events played at one time, in one place. The most conspicuous event was the professional "World" championship, which featured the biggest total purse and first-prize money ever offered in the history of the game. In 1953, the winner of the Tam O'Shanter "World" earned $25,000, twice as much as the *total* purse of all other tour events of the time. Also on offer to the winner was $25,000 for playing a series of exhibitions around the world to help promote George S. May International.

In this way, May used golf to develop his primary business. But he also created enormous interest in golf among the general public. Indeed, it was May's purse money that attracted the attention of the

ABC network, which in 1953 was just getting off the ground and looking for ways to gain viewers. The "World" purse prompted the network to produce the first live national telecast of a golf tournament. When ABC called May and told him they wanted to televise his "World" championship, he jumped at the chance even when told he would have to pay ABC $32,000 for the privilege. An inveterate entrepreneur, May understood the exposure value of the new medium, and didn't mind paying the fee. Of course, he never did again.

In August 1953, May's tournament was telecast across the nation, and with only 15 minutes of airtime left, Lew Worsham holed a 105-yard wedge shot for an eagle two on the last hole to win the first prize. Over a million people saw the fabulous shot, easily the largest single audience for golf in the game's history. Moments after Worsham's wedge shot was holed the ever-extravagant May announced that the first prize the following year would be doubled.

The expansion of golf took a giant leap forward thanks to George S. May's enterprising nature and free-spending style. His adventurous and highly successful innovation in 1953 led the United States Golf Association to begin its annual national network telecasts of the U.S. Open the following year. This was followed soon after by telecasts of numerous regular PGA Tour events, then annual network telecasts of the Masters tournament, the PGA Championship, and ultimately the British Open. Then, the made-for-television specials such as *Shell's Wonderful World of Golf*.

Monroe Spaght was another business executive who liked his golf and also used it for commercial ends that broadened both public awareness and acceptance of the game as well as his company. In 1960, Spaght was the president of Shell U.S.A. He was the first American to head up a group of the parent company, Royal Dutch Shell. A San Franciscan trained as an engineer and researcher in the energy field, Spaght was a member of the Sleepy Hollow Country Club, a tradition-bound golf club in Westchester County not far from American golf's quasi-official birthplace, Yonkers, New York. It was at Sleepy Hollow, following a Sunday round in the summer of 1960, where

Monroe Spaght, a dapper, sophisticated San Franciscan and an avid golfer, was the initiating spirit behind Shell's Wonderful World of Golf. *He was president of* Shell U.S.A. *in 1960 when he conceived the notion that a golf competition played on courses around the world would enhance the image and expand the financial well-being of his company. And give the game of golf a grand exposure.*

Spaght had the brainchild that would become *Shell's Wonderful World of Golf.* While having lunch, Spaght watched "All-Star Golf" on television. This was the first made-for-television golf program. Joe Jemsek and Pete DeMet produced it out of their hometown, Chicago. Jemsek, the owner of a number of public-fee golf courses in Chicago, was then and would always be one of the most distinguished of American public golf course operators. His Dubsdread layout at Cog Hill Golf Club, in a west suburb of Chicago, would become the permanent home of the annual Western Open. He also welcomed touring pros taking a break from the circuit who needed a place to play and practice, and when any of them—men and women—needed a few dollars to tide them over until their putts began to fall, Joe opened his wallet. With "All-Star Golf" he made another dynamic contribution to the growth of the game.

DeMet was a local automobile dealer, and producer of a bowling tournament for television with a format that would be adapted for "All-Star Golf." The Jemsek/DeMet golf show featured 18-hole stroke-play matches between top players of the day, such as Sam Snead, Cary Middlecoff, Tommy Bolt, Bob Rosburg, and many others. At first, they competed on the Jemsek-owned St. Andrews course, but eventually the matches were played on courses around the country. Being a pioneer in the field of televised golf, "All-Star Golf" did not have the most elegant production values. Much of each match was covered by voice-over descriptions of the action accompanying rudimentary artwork of the hole. Simple line overlays showed the flight and position of the shots played. As Jemsek himself once said, "Going in, we didn't know anything about where to put the cameras, how to pick up the ball in flight, and so on. We were making home movies."

Monte Spaght, a sophisticated man of the world who played the saxophone, had a taste for gourmet cuisine and an eye for beautiful women, liked the idea of "All-Star Golf" but only as an idea—golf on television. He thought it could be much better produced, for one thing. Also, having played golf all over the world he thought he could combine the game's international dispersion with a reminder of Shell Oil's worldwide presence. Spaght made comments to that effect to his playing partners on that eventful day at Sleepy Hollow: Gordon Biggar, vice president of public relations at Shell U.S.A., and Vic Armstrong, senior vice president of Kenyon & Eckhart, Shell's public relations agency.

Apparently, Biggar and Armstrong assumed Spaght was just speculating or ruminating, and didn't take his remarks seriously. However, when a few weeks later Spaght asked Biggar and Armstrong how they were doing with the golf show idea, the two men quickly got on their horses.

Was Spaght simply out to produce a better golf program that satisfied his own sense of the game's history and beauty? Yes, to some extent. But he also had considerations that were not quite as romantic. He saw the program as a way for Shell to reach the social and cultural strata with which golf had been long associated—to wit, monied people with a college education, doctors and lawyers, business executives, et al., who for starters owned at least one automobile and probably two. Spaght was already working along this path by other means. He was behind the development of a Shell-sponsored radio program hosted by Leonard Bernstein, the then young and popular new conductor of the New York Philharmonic Orchestra, called *Children's Concerts.* This was the forerunner of the widely acclaimed program of the same kind that Bernstein would do on television, and which Shell also sponsored. Spaght reckoned that a smartly produced golf program tailored to his target audience would fit nicely into this overall concept, reaching what has come to be called a desirable demographic profile. In fact, when *Shell's Wonderful World of Golf* first appeared it was part of a 13-program winter series sponsored by the Shell Oil Company that included eleven *Wonderful World of Golf* shows, and two Bernstein *Children's Concerts.*

As another mark of the unassertive thrust of the show, the commercials never shouted at viewers the specific benefits of its gasoline and oil, and their price. The commercials sold the company itself, its

(Counterclockwise) In foreground left, Gordon Biggar, the head of Shell U.S.A. Public Relations, who was a primary force in the implementation of Monte Spaght's idea for a televised golf program; Mary Sarazen (Gene's wife); Vic Armstrong, who handled the Shell account for his advertising agency, Kenyon & Eckhardt; George Rogers, the announcer for the first four years of the show.

image. It is known in the industry as institutional advertising, or in jargon, soft sell. While Shell certainly expected to sell gas and oil via this golf show (and it did—sales were estimated to have increased by some 30% over its nine-year run), the idea was to do so without a hammer.

Along that same line, Spaght used the program to do some internal public relations. It was a venue by which he could massage service and materiel providers such as oil drilling and refining groups, marketers, and local and regional Shell executives. By inviting them to the filming of the matches and evening parties before and after, he generated considerable goodwill and corporate loyalty. Much good feeling for the company, and perhaps some unpaid overtime work, is developed when a manager of a refinery in Elizabeth, New Jersey has dinner, drinks, and a mingle with television executives who produce a sports television program, and famous golfers. Furthermore, by filming matches in countries that produced oil or were heavy users of petroleum products, and in which business or political problems existed, Spaght could improve those situations by featuring on television the splendors of Venezuela, Spain, Japan.

The first thing Biggar and Armstrong did to move the golf show idea forward was contact film and television production companies in New York City. One of them was Filmways, Inc., which was headed by Martin Ransohoff. Ransohoff, a onetime car salesman, was a low handicap golfer but he had a good track on the job mainly because his company had produced an advertising campaign for the Ford Motor Company based on the popular movie, *Around the World in 80 Days.* The Ford commercials were shot on location around the world, which gave Filmways considerable experience in dealing with customs officials and, in general, the exigencies of working in foreign countries.

As for Ransohoff himself, he didn't think the golf show idea had much merit. He may have been distracted by the fact that at the time he was getting ready to branch out from making commercials to producing feature films. He had his mind on 'going Hollywood.' (His first feature was *Boys' Night Out,* a big hit that permanently changed his career into a full-time movie producer.) Still, the Shell project was a piece of business and when Ransohoff returned to his office after a meeting with Biggar and Armstrong he called in one of his staff producers, Fred Raphael. Raphael, who for 12 years had worked in television commercial production for the J. Walter Thompson advertising agency, remembered that the first thing Ransohoff asked him was if he had a handicap. Raphael, who grew up in a tough neighborhood in Union City, New Jersey, thought his boss meant a problem with a leg or arm. In short, he knew absolutely nothing about golf.

Fred Raphael, the original executive producer of Shell's Wonderful World of Golf, *and for the last five years of the program the producer and director. A few years after the Shell show ended its run, Raphael put together an idea he had conceived in 1963 for a tournament for past champions and other notable professional golfers over 55 years old. It was called the Legends of Golf, and was so successful on television that it led directly to the development of the Senior PGA Tour.*

A problem? After some thought, Ransohoff considered Raphael's very ignorance of golf might be just what was needed. He wouldn't be tempted to improve his own game, for one thing. He assigned Raphael the job of putting together a presentation for the Shell and Kenyon & Eckhardt people. It was a decision that turned Raphael's career onto an intriguingly new and lucrative path.

In preparation for his presentation Raphael read as many golf books as he could find in the public library. He also got the gist of the Shell company's business style, and what Monroe Spaght had in mind for his show. Out of this research he came up with a concept title that was predictable for the time—Around the World with Golf and Shell—and accompanied it with a world map on which pins were stuck in what were considered then, in the days before jet air travel condensed the world, some of the more distant and fascinating countries on the globe. The title didn't work, but Raphael's enthusiasm, colorful presentation, and Filmway's experience filming the Ford commercials won the contract. Raphael was named executive producer.

With the idea now very much in the works, Shell and K&E got more deeply involved in the project's particulars. In view of Raphael's lack of golf background, they hired Herbert Warren Wind as the show's golf writer/ consultant. Wind had already developed a reputation as a foremost golf writer and historian. He wrote the golf for *Sports Illustrated* magazine in its first year of publication, had written a monumental history of American golf—*The Story of American Golf*—and coauthored Ben Hogan's famous instruction book, *Five Lessons: The Modern Fundamentals of Golf.* He also helped Gene Sarazen write his autobiography, *Thirty Years of Championship Golf.* When Shell called on him, Wind was writing golf (and tennis) for *The New Yorker* magazine, which he would continue to do until he retired in the mid 1980s. Wind was a Yale graduate with a formal, courteous manner. He almost invariably wore conservative tweed jackets with a shirt and tie and woolen caps on the golf course, even in summer. In all, he had exactly the golf attitude, style, and knowledge of the game to develop Monte Spaght's concept for the golf show.

Wind would make important suggestions as to the courses around the world that should be used for the matches, the competitive format—18 holes at stroke-play to be sure even a one-sided contest would comfortably cover the time—and players from the countries visited that would provide the best competition. Not many American golf writers, and certainly few fans, knew as Wind did of the Belgian star, Flory Van Donck, Italy's Ugo Grappasoni, or New Zealand's Bob Charles. Wind also suggested Gene Sarazen to be the host of the show. Monte Spaght agreed that was a good idea and Wind made the telephone call to Sarazen.

Gene Sarazen, who died in 1999 at the age of 97, led a very long, productive, and interesting life. A first-generation Italian-American born in 1902 in Harrison, New York, his immigrant father, Federico Saraceni, was a carpenter who struggled to make a living in the New World. He and his wife, Adela, had two children, a daughter named Margaret, and a son named Eugenio. (Eugenio Saraceni changed his name to Gene Sarazen when he was in his late teens and had become a professional golfer. He did so, he often said, because "Saraceni sounded more like a violin player than a golfer." There may also have been the urge to assimilate into American society, which was fairly common among "ethnic" Americans, for he also turned Eugenio into Gene.)

Sarazen never finished his elementary education. He left grammar school in order to earn money and help support the family. He did this mainly by caddying at private golf clubs in Westchester County, New York, first at the Larchmont Country Club, and then the Apawamis Golf Club. Caddying was Sarazen's introduction to the game of golf, and was the starting block for a hugely successful and storied career in the game. But he came close to dying before any of this could happen.

At the age of 14 Sarazen came down with empyema—pus in the plural cavity, as he described it, in *Gettin' to the Dance Floor; an*

Oral History of American Golf. He added: "It...was when I was working at Remington Arms, in Bridgeport [Connecticut]. I was the first case recorded where they sawed the rib, put in a tube and blew water in there to push that stuff out. Every morning....But it didn't look like I was going to make it, at first...There was no such thing as sulfa drugs or anything, then. I remember lying in the hospital and these priests would come in and pull the curtain around. They figured I was going to go."

By way of recuperating it was recommended that Sarazen find work out-of-doors. A friend with whom he caddied at Apawamis, and now a golf professional, Al Ciuci, found him a job as an assistant clubmaker for George Sparling, the pro at the Brooklawn Golf Club in Bridgeport. Sarazen got to play regularly, showed considerable talent, and soon began to outplay his boss. Sparling was not put off. He helped the youngster get even better. Two years later Sarazen took a job as assistant professional at a club in Indiana. He also began to test himself in competition against the best players in the game. He qualified for the U.S. Open in 1920 and 1921, tying for 30th in the former, and finishing sole 17th in the latter. In 1921 he gained some notoriety by defeating the highly ranked Jock Hutchison in an early round of the PGA Championship. The following winter Sarazen won the New Orleans Open. Later that year—1922—in the U.S. Open, at the Skokie Golf Club outside Chicago, he outplayed Bobby Jones, John Black, and Bill Mehlhorn with a final round 68 to win by a stroke over Jones and Black. At the age of 20, he became the youngest winner ever of the national championship. Later in 1922, Sarazen capped his remarkably quick ascent onto the national golf scene by winning the PGA Championship.

Because the star of the era, Walter Hagen, decided not to defend his PGA title in 1922, a special 72-hole "world championship" match was staged between him and Sarazen. Hagen was not only the best player in the game at the time, the wily star was considered especially good at match play. He knew a thing or two about getting under the psychological skin of his opponents, sometimes with a

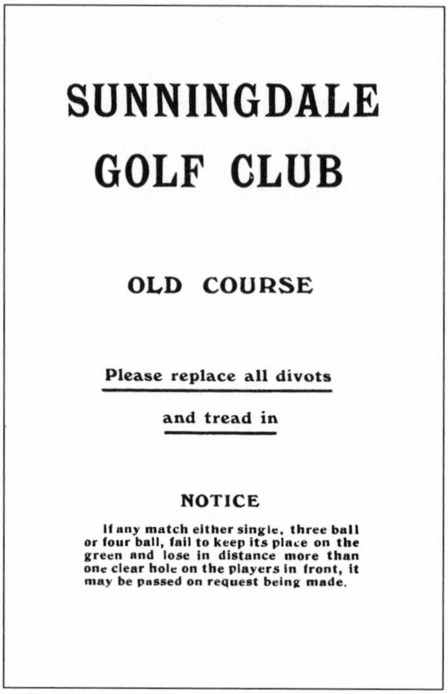

**SUNNINGDALE
GOLF CLUB**

OLD COURSE

Please replace all divots

and tread in

NOTICE

If any match either single, three ball
or four ball, fail to keep its place on the
green and lose in distance more than
one clear hole on the players in front, it
may be passed on request being made.

remark, other times with miraculous recoveries from trouble spots. With the young Sarazen, 10 years his junior, Hagen was up against a different species of competitor than he had ever known. Sarazen often said in later years that he had nothing to fear on a golf course, after having come through his near-death experience as a youth. Indeed, Sarazen defeated Hagen, 3 & 2 in the special match and was now at the pinnacle of the game.

One of Sarazen's most famous quotes was, "Miss 'em quick," and he was indeed a golfer who did not tarry over the ball. He made his decision for each shot—club selection, trajectory, etc.—took the club in hand, gave it a couple of waggles, and swung away with considerable energy. He played golf aggressively, not unlike Arnold Palmer would play when his time came.

Sarazen successfully defended his 1922 PGA Championship title, again defeating Hagen in the final, at the Pelham CC, in Pelham,

New York. Although this was very near where he had grown up, and where his parents still lived, Sarazen's father refused to come onto the grounds of the Pelham club to see his son play. It was a class thing; the Italian workingman did not feel comfortable in the company, however impersonal, of what he saw as the American aristocracy. Neither was the senior Saraceni convinced his son should be playing golf; he had wanted him to become a carpenter. In this case, father did not know best.

The pro tour in those early years of American golf did not offer much in the way of prize money. It was an abbreviated circuit, at best, with only some 20 tournaments a year. Some were at only 36 holes, and almost all were played in the winter. Sarazen made his main living playing exhibitions. Hagen did the same, but without the backup of a club job that gave him a regular salary. Sarazen was a little more judicious. Like Hagen, he had no intention of standing on a lesson tee for six or more hours a day to earn his keep. However, he did take positions as what would now be called the director of golf. He was always free to travel out to play in tournaments, and make his well-paid exhibition swings.

Sarazen never considered himself a tour player in the sense that he went from town to town for seven or eight weeks in a row playing 72-hole tournaments for a $2,500 or perhaps $5,000 total purse. First prize averaged around $500, not even half of what could be earned for a one-day exhibition. Still, between 1922 and 1930 Sarazen won 22 such "tour" events, including the Western Open, which was in his day considered a major title. Of the 22, Sarazen won an amazing five consecutive Miami Opens, another event in the 1920s and '30s considered having major status. To this day, Sarazen and Hagen are the only golfers to ever have won a particular tournament five times in a row.

But it was the U.S. and British Opens which produced the reputation that secured the most lucrative exhibition schedules, and those championships were Sarazen's main goals every year. Alas, although he was almost always a serious contender, after 1922 none came his way for quite awhile. In his first try at the British Open, in 1923 at Troon, he failed to qualify. It was a costly failure both to his ego and his pocketbook. It also reflected on a game that ran hot and cold. He determined his inconsistency was the consequence of a poor grip, in particular the right hand, which he held well under the shaft (the palm up). It is a beginner's grip, and while he may have won important championships with it, Sarazen reckoned with admirable sagacity and honesty that he did so because he had such a stout competitive nature, was able to handle pressure situations, and also because he was a very good putter.

Therefore, in the mid 1920s Sarazen changed his right-hand grip. He turned his right hand to the left until it was "on top," the vee formed by the thumb and forefinger pointing approximately at his right shoulder—the classic position. It was the way Jones, Hagen, Mehlhorn, and all the other fine players of the day placed the right hand. Sarazen figured, correctly, that that was what he needed to do. To orient what is in golf one of the most difficult things to do—change your grip—Sarazen hit on the idea of swinging a weighted club. He got the notion after talking with Ty Cobb, the great baseball player. Cobb spoke about the value of swinging an extra-heavy bat before stepping up to the plate, and Sarazen found that when he swung a heavily weighted golf club with his new grip his right hand had to stay in position in order to complete the swing properly. He poured lead into the heads of a number of wooden clubs and had them situated all around his house and farm in Connecticut, where he was then making his home. He could pick one up anytime, anywhere, and swing it a few times. It worked. His shotmaking consistency improved significantly, and the snap-hook that too often cropped up to bedevil a good round was sent to pasture.

Not long after that progress, Sarazen devised the sand wedge that would be, even in his own mind, his most valuable contribution to the game. It is generally conceded that the sand wedge Sarazen designed has cut the handicap of every golfer in the world by two or three shots. Sarazen came up with the idea because he played poorly

Mr. and Mrs. Sarazen on location in Hamburg, Germany, in 1964.

out of greenside bunkers—as did everyone else, from Sarazen, Hagen, and Jones on down.

There was a sand wedge that preceded Sarazen's, invented by a Texan named McLain. It looked something like a ladle used in steel manufacturing plants—a round back and a concave face. Bobby Jones used a McLain sand wedge during his Grand Slam year. However, the next year it was declared illegal because of the concave face, which allowed the ball to be hit twice with one swing.

Sarazen's sand wedge featured a heavy flange angled in such a way that the back of it struck the sand before the club's leading edge. This meant there was far less chance of the club digging too deeply into the sand, which happened so often with the thin-bladed niblick everyone used at the time. With his wedge, the club's first contact was with the sand behind the ball. Also, being heavier than the standard golf club, it would glide under the ball at just the right depth. The hail of sand itself contributed to throwing the ball up and out of the bunker. And of course, it had a perfectly flat face, which made it legal.

Sarazen's timing was, as always, very good. His improved grip and the sand wedge came during a period when times had gotten tough. The Great Depression that followed the 1929 Wall Street crash had wiped out most of Sarazen's investments and savings. The 1932 British Open was coming up, but he was hesitant about making the trip because of the expense, which couldn't be recovered in full even if he won. Gene's wife, Mary, convinced him he had to go. She told him that with his new grip and sand wedge he could win it. Mary found some money for the journey, and it paid off. In his practice rounds, Sarazen was regularly getting up and down from the bunkers so often that people began asking after the "weapon" he was using, which appeared different. Concerned that officials of the Royal & Ancient Golf Club of St. Andrews might ban the club if they had a good look at it, Sarazen took it back to his hotel every evening hidden under his overcoat. He figured that once the tournament got under way they couldn't ban it. Sarazen won the 1932 British Open, at Prince's, in England, finishing five shots ahead of MacDonald Smith. The sand wedge had a lot to do with his victory.

There was more to come in Sarazen's fabulous career. For instance—The Shot! In the last round of the 1935 Masters, Sarazen came to the par-5 15th hole trailing Craig Wood by three shots. Wood had completed his play, and it appeared he would be the winner. Then Sarazen pulled out his 4-wood to play his second shot. He took the ball out of a low lie with his characteristic, compact, powerful swing. The ball bore toward the right corner of the green, landed just short (there is a bunker there now in which his ball would have landed), it kicked to the left and ran dead into the hole for a double-eagle two. A phenomenal stroke of both talent and luck. Still, Sarazen needed to par in to tie for the title. In this he showed his real spunk, for now he knew exactly what he needed. And he got it. Three pars. The next day he defeated Wood in a 36-hole play-off—the only one at that length in Masters history—144-149. Over the entire 108 holes

During a break in shooting in Manila, in 1962, Sarazen takes a moment to cool off a bit without the jacket he always wore on camera.

it took to win, Sarazen was six-under par. He won the $1,500 first prize, and a crystal bowl for his double-eagle.

As it turned out, when the Masters and British Open supplanted the U.S. and British Amateur championships as major titles, Sarazen became the first golfer to have won the four modern, professional majors—the U.S. and British Opens, the Masters, and PGA Championship. It is generally accepted that his 4-wood hole-out helped to make the Masters tournament the revered event it has become, if not at the moment, certainly in years to come when the tournament's promotional machinery got into higher gear.

Sarazen was 33 years old when his miraculous Masters shot and victory was pulled off. That same year, 1935, he won two more tour tournaments, the Long Island and Massachusetts Opens. But, as noted earlier, he was not one to follow the circuit to all the little towns and small cities where events were scheduled. He played his exhibition schedules, and with a keen sense of marketing had a way of picking the right partner at the right time. In 1935 he went on the road with the celebrated Mildred "Babe" Didrikson (later Zaharias), who in 1932 was a smashing success in the Summer Olympics. In '35 she announced she was interested in golf, and she and Sarazen went out together to show off her ability. The tour drew exceptionally well, despite the hard economic times.

In the 1940 U.S. Open, Ed "Porky" Oliver was disqualified after turning in a score that would have tied him with Sarazen and Lawson Little for the title, because he began his last round before his official starting time. After Sarazen lost the play-off to Little, 73-70, he took Oliver on what was called a Sympathy-for-Oliver exhibition swing. It drew well. The '40 U.S. Open performance was Sarazen's last hurrah in competitive golf, although he did win the 1941 Miami International Four-Ball with Ben Hogan as his partner.

Afterward, Sarazen essentially retired from tournament golf. He had amassed a total of 38 victories. When World War II began, Sarazen made USO tours for the benefit of the American military. He also sold his dairy farm in Connecticut and bought a 300-acre farm in Germantown, New York, where he grew apples, corn, and grapes. To supplement his income he did public relations work for various corporations, in particular Martin-Marietta. However, for all his accomplishments in the game, by 1960 Sarazen's name had pretty much fallen into the mist of time. Then came the phone call from Herbert Warren Wind.

Sarazen recounted the moment: "The greatest break of my life happened one day in 1961 when I was up in the hay field on Mountain Range Farm loading bales onto a trailer. I saw Mary driving up in a car and noticed that she was going faster than normal. She pulled up and told me that Herbert Warren Wind wanted to talk to me on the telephone, and that it was important.

"I figured he just wanted a story, and I wanted to keep working, but Mary said he needed to talk to me right away. When I got to the phone Herb asked, 'How would like to be on a television show?'

"I said, 'Me, I'm no actor.'

"'No, you'll be a commentator,' Wind told him. 'You can host the show. Why don't you come down and give it a try?' So the next day I went down to New York City and had a tryout at the ad agency. They gave me the job. I thought it would only be for one year, but it ended up being for nine."

Gordon Biggar, an imposing man in height, heft, and personality, was the on-the-ground force behind the early development of *Shell's Wonderful World of Golf*. He had one of the greatest players of all time as a host for the show, and one of the most prestigious golf writers to help produce it. That was not enough, though. While he was sure Sarazen and Wind would be very helpful in recommending American players for the show, and courses around the world, Biggar felt more was needed in the player department. To that end, he hired Fred Corcoran as a consultant. Corcoran had been the manager of the pro tour in its earliest years, succeeding Bob Harlow in the position in 1935 and holding the job for the next 15 years. As the tour manager he was responsible for arranging travel and hotel accommodations at reasonable rates for the pros, finding sponsors for tournaments, currying the favor of sponsors already on board, and promoting the circuit in any way he could. In this he showed his cre-

Herbert Warren Wind (left) and Henry Cotton, the great British champion, having a chat during the filming of the 1962 Cotton-Sarazen match at St. Andrews Old Course. Wind was the first writer on the Shell show. He was instrumental in bringing Sarazen in as host, helped create the competitive format, suggested courses around the world on which to play, and foreign golfers to match up against the American golfers.

ative side. For instance, one day when the tour was in Chicago Corcoran got Sam Snead out to Wrigley Field to hit a 2-iron over the centerfield scoreboard. It wasn't that difficult a shot, but the people in the stands didn't know that and were astounded. Some 60 years later John Daly would perform a similar act in another major league ballpark.

Corcoran became Sam Snead's business manager the first year Sam came on the tour, in 1937. He played no small role in developing

Sarazen with Fred Corcoran, the fabled golf promoter, one-time manager of the PGA and LPGA tours, business manager for Sam Snead and Ted Williams. Corcoran was hired by the Shell Company to get the best American pros to play on the show.

and plugging the good-old-country-boy character that made Snead a gallery favorite. In all, Corcoran was a personable Boston Irishman with a common touch, a gift of gab, promotional genius, and the clout among the players to get the best of them to appear on the Shell show. To be sure, Sam Snead played often during the show's run, but that was not merely because he had an "in" with Corcoran or vice versa. Snead was one of the marquee players of the period, and would be for the rest of his long life.

Corcoran was persuasive in getting Ben Hogan to make his one and only made-for-television appearance as a player. He was aided and abetted by a substantial appearance fee—$25,000, Fred Raphael mentioned many years later—but if Corcoran had not been the messenger of that arrangement Hogan may not have come on. No other golfers received appearance money to play on the show, but Hogan demanded it and got it.

In retrospect, it would seem that there should not have been much of a problem getting any of the pros to play a Shell match. They received an all-expenses-paid trip to a foreign land, which one thought would be a pleasant adventure. And they could earn $2,000 for winning the match, $1,000 if they lost, and $1,500 for a tie (the purse rose in subsequent years to $7,000 — $4,000 to the winner, then even higher when the format changed in the last two years). For the time, it was a nice piece of money. But the pros of that era were not enthralled by a long plane ride to a place where English was not always the first language, or even the second, and where it was hard to come by a decent steak for dinner. What's more, the matches were filmed in the summer, right in the heart of the pro tour season, when the best and most lucrative tournaments were played. They would miss a tour stop with a potential $12,000 first prize. Also, a trip to Italy or New Zealand would upset their routine, not to say their body chemistry, which would affect them when they finally did get back to the American circuit. Legitimate concerns, actually. However, the commercial value of an appearance before five or six million televiewers, in terms of potential product endorsements and job opportunities, was a definite value. One of Corcoran's tasks was to convince the best players of the time of these potential advantages from playing on the Shell show. In due time, the players caught on themselves to such benefits. Dave Marr, for example, used his appearances on the Shell show to propel himself into a long career as a television commentator.

Hal Power, a Shell public relations executive who doubled as the still photographer on the golf show, remembered that Monte Spaght told Biggar it was imperative that he get St. Andrews Old Course and Pine Valley for venues for the show in the first year. He hinted that if this didn't happen he might consider not going forward with the program. Spaght was a golf classicist, which was one reason he was prompted to demand that these two prestigious courses be on the schedule. But he also felt they would radiate the elite tone he wanted for the program.

Sarazen was an important factor in getting these courses for the show. Indeed, in the long run his importance to the success of the program cannot be measured only by his presence on camera. Just as vital was his reputation as one of the greatest champions in golf history. He was a factor in Biggar's success in procuring St. Andrews, and in the quest to film a match at Pine Valley. The latter was especially difficult. It was (and is) a notoriously exclusive club that has never sought national championship competitions. It has hosted only two in its long existence—the 1936 and 1985 Walker Cup Matches. But because the club has a deep devotion to and respect for the history of the game, Sarazen's participation in the Shell show swayed Pine Valley's all-powerful secretary at the time, J. Arthur Brown, to okay the project.

One of Sarazen's most important contributions to the life of the Shell show was when, after the first year of the series, Jim Cox, president of the Cox Network, said he was going to drop it from his schedule. The show's first-year ratings were not impressive, and Cox planned to replace it with movies. However, Sarazen convinced Cox to stay with the show. It was a big save, because Cox's Ohio-based network reached a substantial audience throughout the Midwest.

In a less momentous incident, but one that attests to Sarazen's off-camera importance to the program, he directly intervened to keep the production on schedule for the match between Tony Lema and Chen-Ching-Po. It was played at the Kawana Fuji Course, some 90 miles from Tokyo, where the Matsushita Company had scheduled an important corporate outing on the same day the Shell match was to be played. The Matsushita arrangement preceded the contract with Shell, and Matsushita's executives were not at all inclined to change its long-laid plans. Enter Gene Sarazen, who made an interesting discovery in his first couple of years on the Shell show. That is, he found he was as well known, and perhaps even better known in Japan than in the United States. He couldn't quite fathom why, but it was the case and it helped the show out of a jam. He met with Matsushita's highest officers, gave them a few personalized golf lessons, told stories of his golfing exploits, and padded the public relations excursion by learning how to say "arregato gezmah," Japanese for thank you very much. "He practiced that under his breath over and over," said Hal Power. Sarazen won the day, and the golf course. The production stayed on schedule.

It is worth keeping in mind that the Shell show was produced during the 1960s, a turbulent political and social period in American history, not to say the world at large. American university students and not a few of the general citizenry were protesting the country's involvement in the Vietnam war. The United States was still fighting the Cold War, and having problems in Latin America. Finally, the most consequential and tumultuous race-relations conflicts since the Civil War were taking place.

In a few instances the production crew of the show, and Sarazen specifically due to his prominence, came into direct contact with these roiling times. Edna Forde, an Irishwoman who was the script person for almost the entire series, remembered that there was more than a little resistance among factions in the Philippines to having an American film company produce a golf match in their country. "We weren't welcome," Forde said, "but Gene got on the phone with someone and got an okay to play in the Philippines by playing a round of golf with President Marcos [who was a serious golf buff]." Another time, after the match between Gardner Dickinson and Mason Rudolph in Guatemala was completed in 1967 (it aired in 1968), the car in which Sarazen was being driven back to his hotel was confronted by a group of angry, rebellious university students wearing masks and carrying guns. When they slowed the car to a crawl and made menacing gestures, Sarazen rolled down his window and told them in no uncertain terms that he was only a visitor to their country and had nothing to do with their issues. Sarazen had a crisp edge to his voice when perturbed, and it worked here. The students dispersed without making further trouble for him.

The most notable political episode in which Sarazen took part was the time he became an American ambassador-without-portfolio. In 1966, when three matches were being filmed in southeast Asia,

Gene Sarazen, in Rangoon, Burma on a diplomatic mission for the U.S. State Department. He was to play with the Burmese leader, Ne Win, who cancelled out because of an imminent visit from Chou En-Lai, prime minister of Communist China. Sarazen played with the top Burmese professional and other Burmese political figures. They played very early in the morning to avoid the brutal heat of midday. Sarazen was surrounded throughout the match by Burmese military and police officers in mufti, one of whom shot dead a poisonous snake that was scurrying in the rough too close for comfort.

Sarazen was asked by the U.S. State Department to visit Burma and play golf with that country's prime minister, General Ne Win. The administration of President Lyndon Johnson was seeking to improve relations with Burma, even though it was a Communist country. Sarazen was not at all interested, in part because Burma was a Communist country, and also because he was not enamored of Johnson's leadership. However, responding to pressure from the government, from Shell executives, and his own recall of John F. Kennedy's famous line in his inaugural speech—"Ask not what your country can do for you, but what you can do for your country"—Sarazen took on the assignment.

It was a bit scary just getting to it. For fear the plane in which Sarazen was being flown to Rangoon might be shot down by rival military forces, the pilot decided it was safer to land at night and without landing lights. It was not a comfortable touchdown. The golf with General Win was scheduled for 5 a.m. the following morning to avoid the hottest and most humid part of the day. As it happened, Win cancelled out of the game because Chou En-Lai was coming to visit and the Burmese leader did not want to be seen by the prime minister of Communist China playing the quintessential capitalist game. Instead, Sarazen played 18 holes with lesser Burmese officials, and the top Burmese professional golfer. He also gave an instructional clinic, had his picture taken with Burmese officials and others, socialized for a bit, then left. On the first night flight out.

One of Sarazen's most poignant memories of the Burmese golf experience was how closely his foursome was followed by military guards carrying machine guns, and their using those weapons to kill a poisonous snake creeping through the rough nearby.

In the end, despite his initial qualms and personal political orientation, Sarazen was pleased to have done a service for his country. He also took much pleasure from the beautiful ivory box given him as a gift by the Burmese. The episode was concluded later in the year when Sarazen and his wife were invited to a reception given by the President of the United States and Mrs. Johnson for the Chairman of the Revolutionary Council of the Union of Burma, and Madame Ne Win. It was held in Blair House. Also, the round of golf with Win was finally played, at the Burning Tree Golf Club, in Washington, D.C.

There was another moment, much briefer but far more ominous, when Sarazen came face-to-face with the harsh realities of the 1960s political scene. On the trip across southeast Asia from the Philippines to Greece there was a refueling stop at the airport in Saigon, South Vietnam. The American war effort in that country was beginning to build up extensively, and the plane carrying Sarazen and the

Sarazen and George Rogers boarding a Pan Am clipper. The airline, under its dynamic president, Juan Trippe, became the leading international air carrier and was used extensively to transport the production crew to locations around the world. It is estimated the production as an entity logged close to two million miles of air travel during the nine-year run of the series.

European royalty was represented at the match in Belgium by King Leopold and the princess. Sarazen did not seem overawed by this audience, if only because the king and his family were easygoing people.

production crew was told by the pilot that he could not make a normal, long, gliding approach for fear of being shot down by Vietcong soldiers on the ground. The approach was on a short and steep plane, the touchdown harder than customary. "Never again," said Sarazen with some trepidation, as everyone waited in a hangar where, two weeks later, a Vietcong sneak bomb was detonated.

There were also less formal, and far more enjoyable associations with celebrated people that Sarazen had during the run of the show. One was meeting and playing golf with King Leopold of Belgium and his daughter. Sarazen (and everyone else on the crew) also met Grace Kelly when she was Princess of Monaco. She attended the match, which was played on the course at the top of Mt. Agel, high above Monaco. Princess Grace was also at the table for a dinner given for the entire crew and a few Shell customers. Of course, everyone was enthralled by her beauty and her fine but unpretentious manners. At one point during the filming of the match (between Barbara Romack and Isa Goldschmid), the princess remarked to Fred Raphael, who was directing the show, that she was afraid he would not get enough footage of the golf because all the cameras seemed to be trained on her. There was indeed a lot of her in the coverage, but enough golf, too.

Sarazen also helped promote the program with staged photographs that reflected various aspects of a country's culture. Hal Power usually worked these ideas up. In one stint, Sarazen was dressed in a Swiss yodeler's outfit to hit a golf ball off an alpine mountain. In another, he was photographed playing golf in Malaysia, his clubs "caddied" by an elephant. Sarazen was initially reticent about doing these "promos," according to Power, but once he got into them and discovered how effective they were, he became enthusiastic. "He would even contribute to the ideas," Power recalled. "For the golf shot in the Alps, Gene said it could be billed as the longest drive ever hit. He admitted he was a ham, and liked being in the limelight."

More than once, Sarazen remarked how much the Shell show meant to his life and career. But it was also that for everyone else

Sarazen was often called on to do promotional stunts related to the countries in which matches were played as ways to develop more interest in the program. Here he hits a red ball teed up in the snow at the top of an alpine crest near Crans-sur-Sierre, Switzerland. Always a clever publicist, he remarked that he was hitting the longest drive in the history of the game. Certainly it fell the farthest.

A promotional photograph of Sarazen playing golf in Jamaica, his clubs being carried by a Jamaican donkey that was not asked for advice.

who worked on the program. The travel alone was extraordinary; so many places most would never have dreamed of seeing in real life, real time—walking the streets of Kuala Lumpur, ambling through the glistening white birch forests of Nova Scotia, scaling the steps leading up to the Parthenon. The golf itself, although the fuse that lit the show's light, at times seemed to play second fiddle to the globe-trotting side of the production. It had the same effect on the audience, and is what made the Shell show so unique. Thanks to the visionary Monte Spaght and the miracle of television, golf and world travel were fused as they had never been before.

The basic framework of the program had been assembled in New York. But even as the first shows were being produced, people were added (and subtracted), and innovative approaches to filming technique were introduced to the equation. All of which stretched and

In Malaysia, Sarazen had an elephant and a beautiful native woman handling his clubs as he played a shot from light rough.

On the island of Kauai, Sarazen gives a lesson to a local woman.

enriched the character of the program and those who made it happen. The production was far from fixed at the start. It was an ongoing process for much of its life, especially the first five years, if only because televising golf was still so new to the medium. The very first shot out of the box was evidence of that.

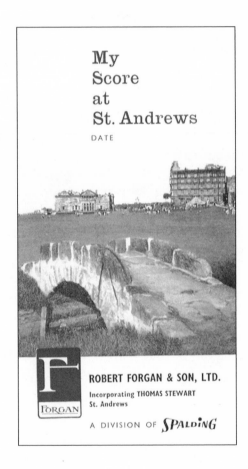

Chapter 2

Show Time!

◆　◆　◆

The very first match filmed for the *Shell's Wonderful World of Golf* series, although not the first to be broadcast, was between Byron Nelson and Gene Littler at the Pine Valley Golf Club, in Clementon, New Jersey. It was a chilly, overcast Monday in early June 1961. Not everyone was completely prepared for the job. In fact, except for the players and Herb Wind, no one on the production staff knew anything about golf other than in passing. This would create a troublesome first act.

Wind's job, aside from writing Sarazen's introduction to the show, which included the golf course's history and a description of the layout, was to instill among the crew a respect for the game's traditions and its manners. "Herb was an adamant golf purist, and sometimes got a little difficult about this," said Dick Darley, who after the Pine Valley match became director and producer of the show. "He eventually became easier with the unusual demands of television," Darley continued.

In the meantime, Wind might have given the crew a brief course in Golf 101, covering the rules of the game and other such basics. If he had, a couple of incidents at Pine Valley might have been avoided that threatened the survival of the show before it ever got past its birth pangs.

The director of the Pine Valley match was Len Goodman, a director of commercials for Filmways, Inc. Fred Raphael remembered taking Goodman and Herb Wind to lunch so the two could get to

In the very first match filmed for the series, Byron Nelson driving from the 6th tee at the Pine Valley Golf Club in July 1961. He played Gene Littler, seen on the right edge of the picture.

know each other, and Goodman could give Wind some idea of what he had in mind for filming the match. Having been told in advance that the director knew virtually nothing about golf, Wind was not overly confident of what was to come. He perked up a little when Goodman mentioned his experience filming Sam Snead. But his enthusiasm dimmed very soon after, when Goodman explained that the filming of Snead was for an Alka-Seltzer commercial.

A screen and television writer named Len Heideman had been hired for his expertise in formatting a television program. Heideman did not know a mashie from a niblick, a divot from a drive. No one on the camera crew at Pine Valley had ever been on a golf course, and therefore, aside from not knowing the fundamentals of how the game worked, the camera operators found it very difficult to follow the ball in flight through their peephole and capture it on film. It was essentially an expertise in the industry that until then had little summons, in any case, and the overcast sky at Pine Valley heightened the problem. As a result, moments after Byron Nelson hit the very first shot in the history of the series, a good drive into the fairway, the cameraman assigned to cover it ran into the fairway and picked up Byron's ball and threw it back toward the first tee. He said he missed the ball, and wanted Nelson to hit another one. Of course, Nelson did no such thing.

That was one of many golf shots the cameramen missed both in flight, and rolling along the ground at Pine Valley. Except for Nelson's opening drive, these coverage failures were only discovered in the cutting room days and sometimes weeks after a match had been played. It was not a good situation for a visual medium in which the ball was, in a sense, one of the stars of the show. To fix the Pine Valley problem, at least, a camera crew was sent back to the course to film struck balls flying in the air, and landing, bounding and coming to a halt. It was not practical to ask Nelson and Littler to return to New Jersey and hit the balls, so Leo Fraser, owner of the nearby Atlantic City Country Club, was brought over for the purpose. He hit only drivers, and was never seen on camera; only the balls that he hit were. The approximate locations where the balls ended up were taken from Herb Wind's notes.

All would have been well had not word of what happened with Nelson's opening drive, and the Fraser subterfuge gotten out to Joe Williams, a widely read sports columnist for the New York *World-Telegram*. The newspaper sportswriters at the time were highly suspicious of television in its early days. They felt threatened by it, for one thing, and in a snippy derogatory tone would refer to those who worked in the new medium as "video jockeys," "space cadets," and the like. Old newsy Williams had a field day with the story of what happened at Pine Valley. He carried on about the illegitimacy of the

Byron Nelson putting in his match against Gene Littler, at Pine Valley GC. Note the sparse "camouflage" in front of the ground-level camera in the foreground. Hiding the cameras became much more elaborate as the series developed. Also note that there was very little gallery out to see the match. That would change, also, as the show gained popularity.

competition, that the TV hotshots made their own rules, etc. etc., and overall implied that you couldn't trust those video jockeys and the stuff they were putting on the boob tube.

From Monroe Spaght on down, the Shell people were stung sharply by Williams's column. It bespoke the antithesis of the image of integrity the program was meant to convey, not only in its approach to golf but how Shell Oil did its business. Actually, there was no breach of the rules. As Byron Nelson recalled: "Yes, the cameraman picked up my ball on the first hole and threw it back to me. But when an outside agency moves your ball, you just put it back approximately where it was and play on; which we did. They made a big stink about it afterward, but it was handled according to the rules of the game.

"Much worse than that," Nelson continued, "was when on the 18th hole I was playing my second shot and in the middle of my backswing the director said 'Cut.' He said the cameras weren't in the right place, or something. Same thing on my next backswing for the same shot. Then again a third time, this one because he was out of film. I finally played the shot, put it in a bunker, and made a bogey five."

Showing a substitute ball in the air and rolling along the ground to where the original actually came to rest was also a very minor discrepancy. No rule was broken here, either, because Nelson and Littler played their actual balls during the match. Nonetheless, image counts and Spaght and Gordon Biggar demanded that Raphael produce a short explanation of the ball-following problems, stressing that there was no intention to deceive the audience. Spaght, Biggar, Williams, and Joe Dey, executive secretary of the United States Golf Association, which reviewed each show for its adherence to the rules of golf, were satisfied with the explanation. It was inserted in the first show to be aired—Dai Rees vs. Jerry Barber, at the Wentworth Golf Club in England, on January 7, 1962. End of the matter, except the story persisted in the annals of the show for its lifetime. (And now, of course, well beyond.)

Immediately after the Pine Valley match, Dick Darley was hired as the director and producer of the program. Raphael remained as executive producer, but during the first three years only occasionally traveled on location. Darley was born and raised in Hollywood, had been in the film business since he was a young man, and began working in television in its incipient years. He directed such popular television programs of the day as *The Millionaire, Space Patrol, Lassie,* and the Rosemary Clooney and Spike Jones shows. He was not a "golf guy," but he wasn't entirely devoid of golf experience. He was a member of the Lakeside CC in Los Angeles, and played now and then. Golf may not have been at the top of his interest list, but making films was and Darley's contributions during his three-year stint on the Shell show were measurable throughout the entire length of the series. "He was very meticulous," said Edna Forde, who Darley had hired during the first year of the program. "Dick was totally dedicated, was a workaholic, and didn't suffer idlers well," Forde recalled.

Even in the exotic landscape of Australia there is no real tree the likes of the one holding the high camera behind a green at the Royal Melbourne Golf Club. Gary Player is hitting a bunker shot in his 1962 match against Peter Thomson.

Darley brought certain production values to the show he thought would enhance it. "I wanted it to look like it came out of Hollywood," said Darley, which is to say, for one thing, that the internal workings of the production were not to be revealed. No one saw the nozzles and pipes creating the rain that fell on Gene Kelly when he danced in it, and no one was going to see the cameras that filmed Sam Snead hitting a drive. To that end, Darley developed a production technique that became something of a talking point for the run of the show, the hiding or camouflaging of the cameras.

At Pine Valley there had been a sketchy effort to hide ground-level cameras with some branches and leaves. Darley expanded con-

Dick Darley at work editing one of the shows. Darley was a Hollywood-trained filmmaker who directed the Shell show for its first four years, during which time he developed many of its permanent production concepts and filming techniques. (Courtesy Edna Forde)

Hal Power (left) and Dick Darley take a coffee and cake break during the filming of a match. Power was a Shell public relations executive who doubled as still photographer on the show. (Courtesy Edna Forde)

A Strange Tree Grows in Scotland. Gleneagles, to be precise. A striking example of the camouflaging of the high camera that was situated behind the greens. The crane and scaffolding was masked with local ground cover, but it still presented an unusual sight to Scottish eyes.

siderably on that. The most dramatic effort had to do with the tower that was mounted on the back of a truck, and on the top of which was a platform that held a camera and its operators. This in itself was a major advance from the camera atop a station wagon for the Pine Valley match. The tower stretched up as much as 50 feet, depending on what was needed for the terrain of each course. The truck itself was usually situated about 15 to 20 yards behind the green, from where the cameraman could cover tee shots and approach shots into the greens. To camouflage the truck and scaffolding, a considerable supply of local foliage was draped on the truck and the scaffold. A Hollywood-trained expert, a greensman, was hired to do the work.

The tower camera presented a fascinating scene on links courses, which are defined to a large extent by their lack of trees. Local Scots who came out to witness the matches played at St. Andrews Old Course, for example, saw an odd-looking growth rising up out of a horizontal landscape on which for all their lives, and maybe a thousand years before—until yesterday—the tallest natural growth was low-lying gorse bushes, or a rabbit up on its haunches. The Scots take their golf seriously, and are not inclined to accept easily any contamination of their holy game and the holy ground on which it is played. But they seemed to take the gawky tower in stride. No one ever saw it on camera, which was the most important thing.

Ground-level cameras were also covered with local tree foliage. But, to be sure they were well-disguised. Darley hired local people so he could move them on command to encircle the cameras. These employees also doubled as gallery, which in some locations represented most of it. During the early years of the program's run there was not a lot of indigenous interest in golf in places such as Morocco, so it could be difficult drawing a true gallery from the local population. On occasion, when a U.S. military base was nearby, soldiers and sailors were invited to see the match. They were asked to dress in civvies, if possible. In countries where there was a film industry, professional extras were hired to be the show's human camera camouflage. This led to some amusing anecdotes.

Darley recalled a time in New Zealand when the crew broke for lunch after eight holes were played. They were at the far end of the course. When lunch was over and the shrouded high-camera truck moved off to the next location, two women were revealed relieving themselves. In Versailles, extras were hired from the French film industry. One attractive young woman who was clearly not aware of the nature of the show she was on, appeared on the "set" as though to play a streetwalker in a B movie—short, tight-fitting dress, spiky high-heeled shoes, no hat. It was a hot day, and at the sixth hole the woman fainted and fell to the turf with a thud. Fortunately, the ground was soft and lush. (So was she, if memory serves.)

The basic production techniques Dick Darley developed would be followed until the end of the program's run. Along with the camera camouflage, he incorporated film-editing techniques such as cutaways to gallery for reaction to the play, and to the announcers, and assigned one camera exclusively to take these pictures. With this footage he could jump through the often long and boring process of golfers getting ready to play a shot. It made them seem faster players than they actually were. The technique also presented opportunities to show an important businessperson or show business celebrity on television for a moment.

The zoom lens was used to enliven the many static situations that prevail in golf. The thrust of the lens somehow put a bit of zip in the methodical waggle, the look to the target and back to the ball. All of that sort of thing is commonplace now, but in the early 1960s they amounted to innovations. When Fred Raphael took over as director, he used religiously what he himself called Darley's production "bible."

Others on the crew made valuable contributions to the show in filming techniques and the editing of the film. Charles Okun joined the crew as a production manager in 1965. His first location was in Osaka, Japan, where Chen Ching-Po and Tommy Jacobs played a match. Okun had a drill sergeant's style, but backed it up with considerable efficiency. He knew how to make a "movie," and get it done quickly without losing quality. After only one day on the show he changed a procedure that made it possible to film an 18-hole match in one day. Until then, an average of 14 holes were played before the light became too dim and production had to stop. The final holes were played the next morning. This was not a comfortable situation for the golfers, who had to rouse themselves out of bed very early, then get loosened up to play three or four holes. Never mind the dis-

comfort this engendered among camera operators and other crew members, many of whom were energetic partying types.

Before Okun came on, all five cameras covering the players hitting their shots did it one player at a time. That meant once Chen Ching-Po, or whoever, hit his shot all the cameras would have to be moved into position for Tommy Jacobs's shot. Okun simply took one camera off Chen and had it already set up for Jacobs's shot. Now a natural and faster flow from one shot to the next was possible. Fred Raphael and the Shell Company liked the change if only because every match could be completed in one day, which brought significant savings in production costs. The players liked it because they didn't have to wait so long between shots. Gene Littler remembered that when he played on "All-Star Golf" the players could hit practice shots in the time it took to set up cameras for the next shot. No doubt with the quasi-rules-breaking incident at Pine Valley in mind, "the Shell people wouldn't let us do that," said Littler. Okun's innovation made it less necessary, and this in turn may have had something to do with the improved play as the program progressed through its run.

The Australian cameraman, Bob Wright, manned the tower camera and became a master at covering the flight of the ball from the moment it was hit until it landed. As earlier noted, there was not much experience at this difficult shot in the industry and Wright helped make it easier for everyone who came after. The problem was always picking up the ball the instant it was hit some 250 or so yards away, then keeping it in the frame as it flew through the air and landed. The telephoto lens Wright had to work with was not as precise as it would become, so he mounted a highly magnified telescope beside his camera's eyepiece. That made it much easier to pick up the ball and take it through its entire trip.

A good thing, too. When Miguel Salas made his hole-in-one in Portugal, a big concern moments after the cheer went up from around the green was whether Wright got the ball diving into the cup. When the director came up to the green with an anxious look at his cameraman, Wright, with a wink and a thumbs up, answered the question. Got it, mate. Not to worry.

Other camera operators, who were increasingly being assigned to cover golf tournaments for the networks and other made-for-television golf shows, picked up Wright's innovation. Wright himself worked for a number of years on the film of the Masters tournament that was (is) produced annually. So did Ed Koons, who Wright mentored and who became the other tower cameraman when, following Okun's lead, two towers were fitted out. This, of course, further speeded up play. It was no longer necessary to move the truck, necessarily slowly, from the first green to the second green and so on, before play could continue. The two towers skipjacked around the course until the match got to the last hole, when both of them covered the play.

One of the most valuable contributions Darley made to the program had nothing to do with filming techniques, but with its content. It was the travelogue segment, which took up about three or four minutes of every program. Darley may not have been entirely responsible for it. Hal Power generated the germ of the idea through the magazine he produced for each year's series, which included pictures and text about the countries in which the matches were played. The travelogue segment was more or less a spin-off of that, but it became an integral part of the television show. It may have had as much to do with the program's popularity as the golf itself, maybe even more, although pure golf buffs would prefer that not to be so.

Red Smith, the iconic American sportswriter, was not much of a golf fan and when asked once how he liked the Shell show replied that he couldn't get terribly excited about a staged contest between Dave Ragan and Celestino Tugot, but he sure liked the travelogues. So did a lot of others.

The travelogue was known in-house, by the production staff, as the Postcard. The name had an interesting coinage that was not mere whimsy. It was actually quite precise. Mack Edwards, who produced and directed the travelogue, didn't have a lot of time to research the countries in which matches were being played. His shortcut, or quick study, was to stop at a local drugstore as soon as he arrived. There he fingered through the postcard rack to find the country's general points of cultural and social interest—Portugal's sardine fishery, Japan's ancient temples, Bahamian straw weaving, Hawaiian folk dances, and so on. Edwards would film those postcard features, add a script that was delivered voice-over, and create a three-minute travelogue—the Postcard.

Also woven through these travel featurettes was the story of Shell Oil operations in the country, including footage of Shell gas stations and other company operations. One of Monte Spaght's aims was to show how worldwide was Shell's retail reach. The Postcard served this purpose, as well as the indirect selling approach he was after. It was an ideal venue by which Shell could project its corporate image while also going about the rather mundane business of selling gas and oil.

The Postcard craftily incorporated the commercials, and was sometimes used as a propaganda tool; propaganda, as in the favorable projection of certain political doctrines. The most transparent

Sarazen rehearsing his opening monologue for the match at the then-new Doral CC, in Miami, Florida. Fred Raphael, on Gene's right, helps Sarazen through the warm-up.

example of this was during the 1962 match, in Hong Kong. It was between the American tour player, Ted Kroll, and Chen Ching-Po, a Chinese from Taiwan who was announced distinctly in the opening of the program as being from "Nationalist China." During the playing of the match, a number of references were made by Sarazen and George Rogers, the cohost and play-by-play announcer at the time, to the fact that Communist China was only a wedge shot away on the other side of a hedge bordering a fairway. This led to brief asides on the virtues of western democracy and the capitalist system, and more than a few mentions of the "bamboo curtain" and the "huge mystery of Red China." There were also pictures of British border guards, and tanks on the highway cutting through the course. In the Postcard itself, portrayals of refugees from mainland China living in Hong Kong hostels were shown cooking their meals in woks heated with Shell kerosene sold for a few pennies and delivered by peddlers described as "free men of private enterprise." Another brief story was told of mainland Chinese orphans attending a school in Hong Kong to learn to be seamen, and that many of them would find employment on Shell tankers. (It was not all propaganda. In this Postcard, for example, we learned that Hong Kong means Fragrant Harbor—a nice little bit of trivia.)

The social and economic strictures of Communist China were disparaged, however subtly, by the Shell Company and its spokesmen. But one did not fool with the powers-that-be at the Augusta National Golf Club. It was in Hong Kong where Gene Sarazen appeared on camera wearing his green Masters jacket. Immediately after the show the stern chairman of Augusta National and the Masters tournament, Cliff Roberts, stiffly reminded Sarazen that the jacket was to be worn only on the premises of the Augusta National Golf Club. Sarazen never wore it again on the Shell show.

The next location after Pine Valley was in Paris, France. Dick Darley took over here as the program's producer-director, and it was when he began to build a permanent production crew. Seven cameras were used for each show, each requiring an operator and his assistant, or focus-puller, in the British lingo. The salaries and travel expenses for an entirely American production crew, all of whom needed to be union members, would be prohibitive. To solve this problem, Darley hit upon the idea of hiring foreign camera operators and assistants as permanent employees to work the entire 11 shows every year.

The foreign cameramen worked somewhat below the pay level of American film union members, but they earned salaries that were

Sarazen, in his Masters jacket, discusses golf with two members of Indian royalty during the match in New Delhi. It was the one and only time Sarazen wore the green jacket on the show. When he appeared on television wearing it he was told by Clifford Roberts, the secretary of Augusta National Golf Club, that the jacket was only to be worn on the club's grounds.

far better than anything they could get in their own film industry. It was for the "foreigners" one of the best jobs financially that they ever had. For example, Vicente Sempio, of the Philippines, was able to buy with money earned on the Shell show a string of jitney cabs, the common taxi transportation in his hometown of Manila. What's more, everyone on the crew received a per diem of $25 to pay their expenses on the road. In the 1960s, prices around the world were such that a prudent person could even save a bit of his per diem money while his salary was being banked at home.

At the same time, in countries where there was a film industry, it was required to hire local production personnel on a temporary, one-shot basis. This included interpreters, bus drivers, grips (who carried heavy objects from one place to another), and a pilot and his helicopter to photograph the course and each hole from the air. The hires in most countries were happy for the work and not especially demanding. This did not include the French, as might be expected. In Versailles for the Ken Venturi, Jean Garaialde match, feisty French production assistants insisted on a French-union-mandated two hour lunch that had to include brie cheese and red wine. Pete Porter, Raphael's production manager, who had an irascible streak of his own, resisted the demands for about an hour. When the French threatened to walk off the "set" and halt production, Porter went shopping for the required victuals and drink. He bargained the Frenchmen down to a house red.

Money did talk. In another incident, Dick Darley recalled that for a Postcard segment in Hong Kong, "we wanted to shoot the women in their conical hats and long black dresses as they cut the fairways by hand. We were told the women were superstitious and would not want to have their pictures taken because it was stealing their soul. But when we asked the women themselves, they said they would do it for seven dollars."

The full-time production crew numbered around 40. Of that number, once Darley made all his permanent hires, around 12 were "foreigners"—two Filipinos, an Australian, eight Britons, and an Irishwoman. The rest were Americans, among them Hollywood cam-

Fred Raphael holds the Emmy awarded the Shell show, in 1966, surrounded by the entire production crew during a party to celebrate the event. Sarazen is fourth from the right, Demaret is second from the left.

eramen, New York- and Hollywood-based production managers, a writer, and an accountant to deal with various financial matters, including paying local employees in their own currency when the filming ended. The accountant's work also included having readily at hand the tributes paid to customs officials in order to get the equipment into and out of countries, a standard operating procedure in most countries. One did well to not try countering that "tradition."

In his dealings with customs officials Porter kept in mind the story of an American film company that was shooting a feature movie in Spain. There was a problem getting their equipment out of customs in Madrid. Just what the problem was, was not specified. A worldly production manager told the director that it would require a tribute to free his gear. The director rose up in moral high dudgeon and said he would not sink to such a level. A week went by, and the cost of being idle was becoming astronomical. At last, the director relented. His production manager went to the customs office, was led through some dusty aisles to a far-back room. There a small, sallow Spaniard wearing a green plastic visor, accepted an envelope filled with the requisite funds. In five minutes, the equipment was out of his realm.

Another money episode, with a Keystone Kops flavor, occurred after Spain's Sebastian Miguel made an ace during his match in Portugal against Frank Beard. A prize of $10,000 was on offer for a hole-in-one (Salas's was the only one made in the run of the show), and with one swing of his club Miguel earned a tidy 25,000 Portuguese escudos. Raphael wanted to pay Miguel the money immediately, but the accountant hadn't allowed for this development and had to make a trip to the local bank to exchange American dollars for the Portuguese currency. The hefty stack of bills was put in an attaché case. Jimmy Demaret and Raphael accompanied the accountant, and on the way back to the course they ran into a police roadblock. All cars were being searched for thieves who had just robbed a different bank. As Raphael recalled the incident years later, when it was their turn to be searched by the police he, Demaret, and the accountant were ordered out of the car. Demaret held the attaché case. The police searched their luggage (they were leaving for the airport after delivering Miguel his swag), and patted each of them down. They never bothered to look into the attaché case, though, and a relieved Demaret said afterward that if they had found all that money they would have spent the next 10 years in a Portuguese prison. Jimmy, being from Texas, had a streak of hyperbole about him.

The production of the Shell show was a monumental project. It involved transporting the 40 people on permanent staff, and finding hotel rooms for everyone during the tourist season in places where tourists often traveled. On average, 30 single rooms were required, and five doubles. Two buses were rented to take the crew to and from the golf course. Six sedans were hired, with local drivers, to transport VIPs—Shell executives and friends, the golf pros, Sarazen, et al. Four 4-wheel drive vehicles were needed to transport equipment around the course, and be fitted out with the high-camera platforms. An equipment storage area was needed to store some 30 heavy wooden shipping cases containing the cameras and their tripods and

Sebastien Miguel (far left), made a hole-in-one during his 1968 match with Frank Beard (far right), in Barcelona, Spain, worth $10,000 US.

batteries. Battery chargers were needed. A helicopter was hired at each location for the aerial coverage of the course—those flyovers of each hole that are accompanied by a voice-over description. The Shell show was the first to do this. Lunches needed to be bought for what came to nearly 100 people on location, including the local hires. Interpreters were needed in many locations. This highly involved, complicated, and expensive operation was performed in 11 different countries around the world for nine years. It was a fantastic undertaking, and yet it came off remarkably well. On the whole.

One year, in an effort to save money, and perhaps some inconvenience, Raphael chartered a 4-engine passenger plane to transport the company. It was a turboprop plane, and while it may have been handier in some ways it was much slower in the air. This prompted the longest sustained crew poker game in the company's history—a 14-hour Jacks-or-Better Progressive/5- and 7-card stud and High-Low-Split-the-Pot marathon on the trip back from Norway to New York.

It took three forms of transportation to reach one location, Cape Breton Highlands, on the far eastern tip of Nova Scotia. There was the flight from New York City to Sydney, Nova Scotia, and from there a bus ride of some 100 miles that included being ferried over an inlet of the Atlantic Ocean to Cape Breton Highlands National Park.

The annual budget for the show was in the neighborhood of $1.3 million, which in the 1960s was a significant amount. It didn't increase all that much over the nine years of the show, according to Raphael. However, in the last year or so, by which time Monte Spaght and Gordon Biggar had retired, a lack of enthusiasm for the program arose within the Shell Company. The people who replaced Spaght and Biggar were not golf buffs in their mold, and they decided the money could be better spent on other projects. The Shell Company ended the show, but not because of poor ratings. The people who came to be in charge didn't care about golf. The game, as we said earlier, has always benefited from patrons with influence. The Shell show ran out of them.

The announcer hired to work with Gene Sarazen at the outset was George Rogers, a tall, handsome man with a mellifluous baritone voice, good diction, and an overall well-trained professional style. He had been working as a newscaster on local television stations in Baltimore, Maryland. Rogers did the opening announcements, some of the play-by-play and hole descriptions, and read the Postcard scripts. After Darley left the show, Rogers worked himself into a powerful position as a coproducer. He took on the crucial job of editing the thousands of feet of film shot for each match, and putting together 56 minutes of competitive golf.

However, Rogers became a victim of overweening self-importance. He came to the notion that the show could not go on without him, a malady of many sports announcers. He overplayed his hand with the Shell people, didn't get any help from Sarazen, and was let go after the 1966 series.

Jimmy Demaret replaced Rogers. It was a change that especially pleased Sarazen, who had become suspicious of Rogers. He felt that in the cutting room Rogers was not giving him a good shake, was

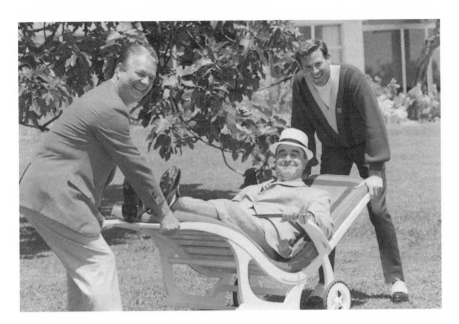

A light moment in Faro, Portugal, with Demaret and Doug Sanders carting the Squire around the hotel grounds. Sanders played Peter Alliss at Henry Cotton's Penina course in 1967.

cutting him out of too much of each show. He also complained that Rogers was hogging the microphone during the matches. On review many years later, Sarazen seems to have had a point. In the famed Hogan-Snead match, Sarazen did not comment on- or off-camera as much as he might have. Sarazen also felt Rogers was instructing the cameramen to shoot him at an angle that made him look even shorter against the much taller Rogers. Most of that was typical show business persnickety, the kind of thing that has gone on among performers forever. But what really put Sarazen off was the fact that Rogers projected himself as a golf expert when he actually had very little background in the game. This was compounded by the fact that Rogers played terrible golf.

Sarazen had no such qualms about Demaret, who had won 31 times on the pro tour, including three Masters tournaments, and was widely recognized as one of the best players to ever come down the pike. Some said he would have had an even better record if he had taken his golf more seriously. Demaret's response was that he wouldn't have done as well if he tried harder, had done the "Hogan thing." Demaret marched to his own drummer, and had a good bit of the show business in him. As a young man just starting out in the world he sang in a nightclub in Galveston. The owner of the club, Sam Maceo, was also one of Demaret's sponsors on the pro tour. That may have been both a measure of Maceo's respect for Demaret's golf game, and a statement about his ability to sing. Actually, Demaret had a rather nice high baritone voice and could croon a tune in style. But he had a much better cut shot, and low ball into the wind.

Demaret had a pleasant smile, laughed easily, and could pitch a wisecrack with the best of them. He liked to tell of the time he traveled the pro tour during the Depression and used an "Oklahoma credit card" to fill his tank; that is, a siphon with which he drew gasoline from someone else's car. When Sam Snead appeared on the show with his newly adopted croquet-style-putting stance, Jimmy said Sam looked "like he was basting a turkey." Another time he characterized it as looking "like a land crab." He called the fringe of greens "frog hair," and really low shots "worm burners." Those terms seem stale now, but Demaret was making them popular (and perhaps coining a few) in the 1960s.

Raphael recognized how much looser Sarazen became now that he was working with Demaret. Once, when remarking on air that Shell would pay $10,000 for a hole-in-one, Demaret added, "And Sarazen will pay $25,000." He got a good chuckle out of Gene with that one. Raphael often tried to get the two of them into a dialogue that might develop a light and humorous air. One of the better results, although not for a family program, was the time in Portugal when Sarazen was prompted to tease Demaret about his big-city background. He reminded Jimmy that they were in farm country. Jimmy said he knew that, and Gene responded by saying, "How would you know, Jimmy, you're a city boy from Houston." To which Demaret replied, "Well, Gene, it's easy to tell. For instance, I know very well that just behind the green over there are almond trees. I know that because of the way their nuts are hanging." Sarazen roared. So did everyone in the editing room. However, the line never saw the light of CBS on Sunday afternoon.

Demaret was good pals for years with Bing Crosby, bandleader and singer Phil Harris, and many other Hollywood personalities. He had no desire whatsoever to steal the spotlight from Sarazen. He had been in it most of his life, and was very self-confident. Ironically, Demaret was the announcer on the very "All-Star Golf" program that drove Monte Spaght to do a bigger and better golf program.

Demaret's most recognizable distinction, aside from his golf talent and flip lip, was his clothes. In particular the colors, which were luminescent bordering on gaudy. He also did some styling in the way of suede shoes and rakish hats. But it was the colorful shirts and slacks that were most notable. In fact, Demaret was the catalyst who changed the way golfers dressed. In the late 1930s he was playing the pro tour and, like everyone else out there, wore fedora hats, shapeless brown pants, white dress shirts, plain black or brown leather shoes. As Demaret once put it, "Everybody looked like pallbearers out there." He decided to do something about the grim fashion style, at least as far as he was concerned.

Demaret's father had been a house painter in the days before motor-driven shakers that mixed colors. He did the mixing on his own, trying out the combinations on the walls of the Demaret home. From that Jimmy said he got his sense of color. One day in the late 1930s he was in a clothing manufacturer's showroom in New York City's garment district, and saw rolls of brightly hued silk material. He said he'd like to get some shirts for golf made from them. When told it was stuff used for ladies dresses Jimmy said he didn't mind at all (one of his few golf instruction dictums was, "Hold the club lightly, as though it was your girl friend"). Some shirts were done up for him. Being a star golfer on the tournament circuit, he was seen widely in his outfits and a revolution in golf wear developed that became a permanent sartorial statement.

However, there was also some function to the form. Not only were the shirts he wore dazzling to the eye, they were cut to be loose fitting so a golf swing could be readily made in them. That, more

In dress style, Sarazen and Demaret reflected two generations of American golf. Sarazen the traditionalist, Demaret the modernist. Note, however, that they are style and color coordinated in respect to their shoes. (Courtesy Dick Ashe)

Sarazen and Jimmy Demaret at St. Andrews in 1967. When the jolly, colorful Demaret replaced George Rogers as cohost, Sarazen's humor improved greatly. Demaret's pixie spirit was somewhat tamped here, though, as the tam o'shanter he is wearing has Shell's Wonderful World of Golf *stitched on the rear. Jimmy meant it to be in front as a billboard, but the Shell public relations representative traveling with the show, following up on the company's understated style, scotched the idea. (Pun intended.)*

than the colors, was one of the more valuable contributions Demaret made to the game.

It was a credit to the Shell Company that it brought in Demaret as an on-camera presence. It proved that Monte Spaght, et al., weren't entirely bound to old golf traditions. At the same time, an occasional rein had to be pulled on Demaret's puckish ways. At St. Andrews Old Course, for example, where Phil Rodgers played Dave Thomas, Demaret showed up on the first tee wearing a bright tam o'shanter with the words *Shell's Wonderful World of Golf* on the front. The Shell public relations man who traveled with the show, Geoff Darlington, quietly told Jimmy that the inscription on the tam o'shanter was not in keeping with the company's sense of decorum.

The boundaries of the course are:
the 3rd hole: The fence on the right and the woods behind the putting green.
the 4th hole: The woods on the right of the fairway (posts indicate the line).
the 7th hole: The fence and the ditch on the left.
the 8th hole: The ditch on the left (posts indicate boundary line).
the 9th hole: The ditch on the left, the car park, and the practise putting green (posts indicate boundary line).
the 12th hole: A ball played over the fence which lies to the right of the fairway and to the left of the railwaylines is out of bounds.
the 13th hole: The fields on the left.
the 14th hole: The fence on the left; the wood and garden behind the putting green.

Too bold. Jimmy was a bit peeved, but agreed to turn the tam around and wear it backward, as it were. To get his druthers, Demaret began to end his introductions to the show, the sign-off after giving the score of the match, and for commercials and Postcard breaks with an exaggerated, "....on *SHELLLL'S Wonderful World of Golf.*"

It took twice as long to edit the series as it did to shoot it. The editing was done in the offices of Directors Group, Inc., the company Fred Raphael and some partners put together about midway through the series and took over the contract from Filmways. Other partners in the group produced commercials. At one time the offices were in a hotel on 7th Avenue, in New York City, where Jackie Gleason's "Honeymooners" series was headquartered. In the barbershop on the street level, mafioso Anthony Anastasia was gunned dead while being shaved. Upstairs in the 1960s, a bit of golf history was being produced.

The editing of the 30,000-plus feet of 16-mm color film that was shot for each match down to exactly the 2,123 feet that aired was in many ways the most creative aspect of the production. It could also be the most frustrating. Time constraints made it necessary to cut golf shots and comments everyone was sure would bring the show another Emmy. But everyone also discovered that once a cut was made no one missed what ended up on the cutting room floor. *Sic transit gloria mundi.*

There were some tricks to the trade. On one occasion the editors absolutely needed a ball in flight for a match being played in Norway. There was nothing to be found with the appropriate blue sky in the Norway footage. A few feet were found in a match shot in Spain, and it was inserted. The fastidious folks at Shell and Kenyon & Eckhardt didn't catch that one (can't imagine how they could have), and neither did any sportswriters. But in the very first show of the series Monte Spaght, while reviewing the final cut, caught a split infinitive. All hell broke loose.

Spaght didn't remember where the split infinitive occurred in the show, but he insisted it be corrected. He told Raphael that he could not have schoolteachers in Wichita writing to the company about it. If it wasn't corrected, Spaght said, the show could not go on.

Raphael had four days to find and eliminate the split infinitive before the absolute deadline for delivery of the final cut to the network. When he told Herb Wind about it, the Yale graduate with honors in Literature and one of the most careful and correct writers one could find, refused to believe he had perpetrated the heinous crime. The search began. Wind screened the material for which he was responsible—the travelogue and the golf commentary. Nothing. Spaght refused to believe it was a figment of his imagination. The search continued.

Raphael hired a professor of English at Columbia University to review the show. He was paid $75, and gave Raphael two looks for the money. He found nothing. The moment of detection came from an unexpected source. Raphael had hired a recent graduate with honors in English as a filmmaking apprentice. One of his jobs was to review the shows for lighting or sound problems. As he set to work on the show in question, Raphael jokingly told him to keep his ear out for a split infinitive. A half-hour later the young man came in saying he found it. Raphael was beside himself. The split was in one of the commercials, which Herb Wind and the Columbia professor did not see or hear because it was not included in the cut of the program that they reviewed. The split was made whole, so to say, and all was well. The split infinitive? "To boldly go where no one has gone before." On with the show.

Eliminating grammatical glitches, producing interesting glimpses of a country's heritage, lifestyle, and traditions in the Postcard, and all the other sidebars to the Shell show gave the program a distinctive tone. It had a sense of refinement not always associated with commercial television then (or now). But in the end it was the golf that sold the program; golf being played in the most unexpected places in the world, golf played by some of the best players in the game, and in more than a few instances by golfers the audience had never heard of and would never have if not for this program. In this, and in all other respects, the audience had a kaleidoscopic television experience.

Sarazen with a maharajah and a maharani during the match in Delhi.

CHAPTER 3

THE MATCHES

◆ ◆ ◆

The first year of *Shell's Wonderful World of Golf* appeared on the Columbia Broadcasting System. But because CBS did not yet have a color broadcasting capability, in the second year the show was switched over to NBC, where it remained for most of the run; ABC got it for one year, and CBS had one more season.

A check back with Nielsen Media Research on the rating of the Shell show is interesting. They were not as high as many now think, given the legendary status of the program. However, they are quite close to what the best-rated televised golf of any kind draws on television 40 years later. A random sampling of ratings for shows from each year of the run indicates an overall consistency, with up and down blips where one might expect them. The very first show aired on January 7, 1962 and got a 5.2 rating, a 15 share, and a total audience of approximately 2,548,000. The show featured Jerry Barber and Dai Rees, hardly marquee names, so the relatively low rating is understandable. The fact that this was a brand-new entry into televised golf and sponsored by a major company seems to have had no impact. Three shows later, though, when the legendary Byron Nelson and then current U.S. Open champion Gene Littler played at the storied Pine Valley GC, the rating jumped to a 7.1, 21 share, a total audience of 3,479,000.

Then again, the January 20, 1963 program featuring Gene Littler and the little-known-in-America British player Eric Brown pulled a 7.5 rating. Perhaps this is because the show was catching on after its first year on air. This was the first match of the second year of broadcasting. And yet, the match shown a month later between two giants of the game, Sam Snead and Jack Nicklaus at Pebble Beach, had the same rating as Littler and Brown.

A 7.5 was the highest rating garnered in the random sampling of 17 shows. The much celebrated Hogan-Snead match, in 1965, drew a 6.6, not quite as good as the 6.8 pulled by that season's opener, featuring Dave Marr vs. Britain's Bernard Hunt. Neither Marr nor Hunt are nearly equal in star value to Hogan and Snead, which suggests that ratings are impossible to definitively evaluate.

Throughout the nine-year run of the show it averaged a 6.0 (based on the 17 ratings we counted), and has a rather neat bookends-type ratings history. It began with a 5.2 (Barber-Rees), and ended with the same number for the very last show in the series, a match between Frank Beard and Dan Sikes. Just as it began with nonmarquee players, so it ended, and with the same audience draw.

The fact that the first year's series didn't get the ratings Shell had hoped for, if not expected, may have been to some extent because it did not appear in color. More likely, it didn't help to introduce the series with a match between Jerry Barber and Dai Rees, two excellent players but not anything close to marquee golfers. It seems in retrospect that the Pine Valley match, with the renowned Byron Nelson and Littler, playing on a legendary course would have been the logical opening act. And indeed, as we showed earlier, it did get a much better rating than did Barber vs. Rees.

In any case, the ratings were disappointing and Gordon Biggar, Shell's public relations chief, brought in Hal Power to see what could be done about generating more interest in the show. One of Power's first efforts was to put on an elaborate media party at Tavern-on-the-Green, the famous restaurant in New York City's Central Park. Power designed the affair after the world-traveling theme of the Shell show, and arranged for an 11-course meal (one for each match in the series), with chefs preparing a dish typical of each country in which a match was being played that year (1962). A gourmet's delight.

"The bill was $15,000," Power recalled, "and when Gordon Biggar saw it he was a little stunned. But everyone seemed to think, afterward, that it was worth every penny. The show began to get more coverage in the press."

The ratings began a small climb afterward, and when the show won an Emmy Award in 1966, its career was made.

Every one of the 92 matches played on the Shell show featured one American professional golfer, who would almost invariably compete against a non-American. There were 11 matches between two Americans, most of them when they were played in the United States. To further amplify the international character of the Shell show, in every country outside the United States the second player would be a native of that country. That was not always easy to accomplish, though. Some countries simply had no one with sufficient ability. Or no one at all. Morocco and Greece, for example, had no professional golfers anyone could find. Luxembourg, Venezuela, and Jamaica were other examples of golf having not yet reached the kind of universality that produced the top-notch players it does now.

When no Venezuelan or Moroccan or Greek professional or high-quality amateur (Ireland's great amateur, Joe Carr, played Al Geiberger in Killarney, and won) was found, Argentina's Roberto DeVicenzo was often called on. DeVicenzo played seven times on the series, once in his homeland, then in Venezuela, Chile, Morocco, Greece, Kenya, and the U.S. Indeed, DeVicenzo made more appearances than anyone else, including Sam Snead, who played six times. Why so much DeVicenzo? Because he was a very good player, for one. But also, in his modest-seeming way and slight mangling of the English language, he was an attractive personality and obviously foreign, or not American.

Still, thanks to the Shell show, Americans had an opportunity to see foreign players who were unlikely to ever appear in the United States after George S. May cancelled his Tam O'Shanter World Championships: for instance, Ugo Grappasoni, Flory Van Donck, Pete Nakamura, Eric Brown, Celestino Tugot, Harry Bradshaw, Jacky Bonvin, Jean Garaialde. Not all the international golfers were top-

The great Irish amateur, Joe Carr, after hitting a shot during his match against Al Geiberger at the Killarney GC, in 1965. (Courtesy Al Barkow)

```
┌─────────────────────────────┐
│                             │
│    KILLARNEY GOLF           │
│    AND  FISHING             │
│       CLUB                  │
│                             │
└─────────────────────────────┘
```

Local Rules

1.—**OUT OF BOUNDS:** (a) All ground out-side palings and fences bounding the course; (b) Tilled ground.

2.—A ball may be lifted and dropped immediately behind without penalty; (a) if it lies in a hole in the course through the green so that a club laid across it in every direction does not touch it; (b) if it lies in its own impression on the fairway.

3.—(a) **HAZARDS** include all sand bunkers and the lake shore.

  (b) The Lake is a lateral water hazard, except when playing the 16th when it is a water hazard.

4.—**ALL ROADS** may be considered ground under repair.

PLEASE REPLACE DIVOTS.

PLEASE DO NOT DELAY UNDULY.

———————————

KILLARNEY PRINTING WORKS, LTD.

drawer players who would be threats in major competitions such as the U.S. and British Opens, or the Masters, but they were in most cases quite competent enough and gave good competition on the shows.

In a few instances a player was found to represent his country who did not quite fill the bill. Fortunately for Jay Hebert, Charles Okun's introduction of production techniques that allowed the matches to be filmed in one day came after Hebert's match in Hamburg, Germany. Otherwise, he might have had one of his most embarrassing moments as a professional golfer. In those days before Bernhard Langer, Germany did not have anyone in the way of a high-quality professional golfer. But Shell wanted a German representative, and Friedel Schmaderer was found to play Hebert.

Schmaderer was a tallish fellow who brought to the party a gentle disposition, and a very short, quick golf swing that had garnered him some success in Germany but nowhere else. It should be added that Germany in the 1960s did not offer up a substantial competitive schedule within its own borders. In practice rounds with Sarazen prior to meeting Hebert, Schmaderer often expressed his awed respect for the legendary champion, who was some 25 years his senior and who easily whipped the young German in the three practice rounds they played. Schmaderer was about a two-handicapper who had to play a Ryder Cupper, winner of six tour events including the 1960 PGA Championship, and the owner of one of the most graceful swings in the game.

The trouble arose when Hebert didn't get into Hamburg until late in the afternoon the day before the match was to begin. He had just completed a tournament in Cleveland, and the flight from the United States took some 10 hours. He was groggy when he arrived, and couldn't play even nine holes on the Hamburg GC layout to familiarize himself with the course. The next morning, still under the influence of jet lag, Hebert was simply not in shape when the bell rang. At one point on the front nine Raphael looked over at Hebert, who was mysteriously very still at the side of the green, and wondered if he had fallen asleep "I do believe e's 'aving a bit of a kip," said George Pink, the British cameraman. He was.

Schmaderer played reasonably well, and after nine holes was two strokes up on the American. At this point, Raphael did his fellow American a favor and gave him a "homer" call. The nine holes were completed at around three in the afternoon, so there was time to get at least three more holes in. But to everyone's surprise Raphael called it a day. He said he was running low on film, and the delivery of more from the States hadn't cleared customs. It sounded logical, and Hebert got a chance to get some much-needed sleep.

Before retiring, Hebert thanked Raphael for the break in the action, but he also asked the producer/director, with a certain degree of panic, if it was possible to buy the film should he lose to Schmaderer. He was worried that his reputation would be sullied by losing to the quick-swinging, no-resumé German. Raphael told him that was impossible, of course, but the next morning Hebert had his body chemistry back in order, birdied the first three holes on the back nine, and won going away. Phew!

As suggested earlier, the production of the Shell shows were at first rather primitive by standards that have since developed. In its day, though, they were not so much advances as they were pioneering efforts, the breaking of new ground. More than a little of what the production crew learned from the seat of its collective pants in filming and editing these early shows together would help improve golf coverage by everyone in the years to come.

The Shell show was the first to use the split-screen technique to compare the golf swings of the players; and slow motion and stop-action to expand and enrich this treatment, especially for the tips on technique that concluded every show. In these sequences golf swing buffs had a rare opportunity to study in detail the swing action of such greats as Ben Hogan and Sam Snead, Byron Nelson, Billy Casper, and so many others. It became an even better study when the films were made available many years later on videotape. Now the swings could be played over and over again at the viewer's leisure.

As noted earlier, in the first four years of the show it took at least two days to film an 18-hole match. But one took six days, according to one of the participants, Jackie Burke Jr., who may have added a few days in the embellishment-of-facts tradition of native Texans. In any case, his match against Canadian Stan Leonard on the Banff Springs course in Canada did run over the usual time frame. The filming took place in September 1961, and the weather was not cooperative. Winter was nigh in the Canadian Rockies, and a light snow fell at one point during the play. Shooting had to be stopped more than once for lack of sufficient light, not to say the chilly air. Leonard was used to such conditions. Burke was not, and was impatient with the situation. Some 45 years later he still remembered well how it went.

"We sat in a car with the heater on between shots, waiting for them to set up the cameras for the next shot we had to play. Or until it stopped snowing. They broke their rule and let us hit a few practice shots in between to keep loose, and warm. One time the director stopped me in the middle of a putt—just about when I was ready to draw the club back—because he wanted to change the camera angle and pick up a mountain stream between me and the hole. Another

Snow fell at Banff Springs, Canada, in September 1961, when the Jackie Burke-Stan Leonard match was being filmed. Sarazen, far right, helped workmen brush snow from a green so play could resume.

time, I had a three-footer and it was snowing and the director said he wanted me to wait to make the putt so he had more light. I said I wasn't waiting anymore, and putted out."

The putt was more or less captured on film—a furry image of someone at golf. A Burke double was not sent back the following spring to hole the putt in good light.

No matches were filmed again that late in the year, even in more salubrious climes. But sometimes the date was immaterial. In Nova Scotia, in June, production was delayed for a day by an "unusual" spring snowfall. Most matches were filmed June through August, and because many were played in the Southern Hemisphere the courses

Stan Leonard putting in the snow during his match with Jackie Burke at Banff Springs. Later in the match Burke had a short putt that the director wanted him to wait on until the snow stopped and there was more light. A chilled Burke gave that idea an equally chilly reception, and putted out.

were not always in the best condition. Which is to say, for one thing, they were not always green. These were the days before worldwide resort golf had become the standard it is now—a standard that rose thanks in no small part to the popularity of the Shell show. Money was not spent to keep these courses luxuriant in the summer months. Thus, in Morocco the match between Robert DeVicenzo and Tom Weiskopf was on brown greens. Jimmy Demaret avoided the oxymoron by calling them "browns," as in, "DeVicenzo has hit this 10th brown, and has about a ten-footer for his birdie." The Shell folk overseeing the programs' content had these descriptives "modified."

In Greece, the Glyfada Golf Club course, which sits at the end of a runway of the Athens airport, became a kind of easel. It was mid-July, and the entire course, the only one in the country and only a year old—was as brown as a pancake. It was decided to fool a bit with nature, and paint the course. Raphael hired a dust-cropper plane, had it loaded with all the green paint one could find in Greece, and

BANFF
Springs
GOLF COURSE

sprayed the layout with a couple of coats. The fairways came up look-ing rather nice. It wasn't Augusta National, but not Moroccan brown either. It looked fine on television.

At other times, nature was left in its natural state. When Fred Raphael arrived at the Southerndown Golf Club, in Porthcawl, Wales to get a first look at the course on which Bob Rosburg would play Dave Thomas, he saw a large flock of sheep grazing the fairways. It was a common practice going back hundreds of years in Great Brit-ain for sheep to pasture on local golf courses. Also, it was essentially how the courses were "mowed." The sheep were kept off the greens by foot-high fences circling the putting surfaces. Raphael's first reac-tion was to say the sheep had to go; you couldn't film a match for

Sarazen and Dave Marr enjoy some Belgian beer in an outdoor café in Brussels in the summer of 1963.

In the summer of 1963 Sarazen and Dave Marr played a practice round over the Royal GC de Belgique, where Marr played Flory Van Donck. In 1965, Marr won the PGA Championship.

Sarazen tees off on the first hole of the Old Course, St. Andrews, Scotland, to begin his 1962 match against Henry Cotton.

television with sheep nipping at the turf. But when others suggested the sheep would make an interesting difference in the show, the wool was pulled from Raphael's imagination. It took a bit of nimble footwork by the film crew to avoid the droppings, and a few inattentive cameramen in their rush to get to the next setup stuck their feet in some dip. But on the whole, the golf at Southerndown had a uniquely ovine background that gave it a special character.

Scotland's weather is always a dodgy affair. Even in midsummer on any given day it can be downright cold, making the ever-present wind all the more dreadful. It was just that for the first match at St.

Sarazen, driving from the 18th at St. Andrews. There was no problem getting a gallery for this match between the legendary Squire and England's revered pre-World War II champion, Henry Cotton.

Andrews Old Course in the show's first season. Gene Sarazen played Henry Cotton. It was a nice touch to bring these two masters from a previous generation together on the celebrated "birthplace" of golf. Cotton was a three-time winner of the British Open, and the best golfer in England and arguably in all of Europe from the mid 1930s into the 1940s. Unfortunately, he and Sarazen had to play in miserable conditions—a vicious wind, temperatures in the high 30s. They donned heavy overcoats between shots and did not score very well.

The matches were not often suspended due to inclement weather, but another time at St. Andrews, for the match between Phil Rodgers and Dave Thomas, the match was suspended after only a few holes were completed. Golf may have been out of the question, but it did not deter some local lads from having a fine frolic in the sea. The writer on the show at the time remembered sitting in his corner room of the Rusack's Hotel overlooking the 18th green and first tee of the Old Course, and the beach just beyond. On the strand he saw a band of Scottish youth in bathing suits. It was 40 degrees, bordering on 35, it was misting rain, and the wind was up. But it was June, which is to say, summer. Summer is when you swim in the ocean, and the bleach white and chapped red, bony figures splashing about in the frigid Firth of Forth remains an astonishing memory.

The advent of the Shell show was well timed in that it was able to get future superstars to appear before they became too pricey to play for a mere $2,000 or even $7,000, and/or had shows of their own. As a result, the Shell show featured the likes of Gary Player and Jack Nicklaus before their superagent, Mark McCormack, developed a television series just for them and Arnold Palmer, called Big Three Golf. Palmer did play on the show when he was well into his fabled career, but while no one can say for certain, there must have been a sound business reason for his making the appearance.

Nicklaus played Sam Snead at Pebble Beach, for the 1963 series, and it became an interesting and somewhat contentious clash of generations. The match was scheduled to begin at 8 A.M., but Nicklaus had been competing in a tour event until the day before and did not arrive at the course until 9:00. He felt he needed to hit some practice balls and otherwise prepare himself mentally for the match. He was ready to go at 11:00.

Snead became restless about being made to wait by the younger man, and so did the producer because the delay was going to cost more money. Pebble Beach had set aside three hours for filming the first day without taking any paying customers. The time ran out just as Snead and Nicklaus hit their first tee shots. They were allowed to

A nice piece of American golf history is portrayed in this picture of Sarazen, Craig Wood, and Demaret during the 1967 match between Arnold Palmer and Julius Boros on the island of Eleuthera, in the Bahamas. Wood was the referee. It was Wood who Sarazen defeated in a play-off for the 1935 Masters, after holing his 4-wood in the final regulation round for a double-eagle on the par-5 15th hole at Augusta National. Wood won the Masters, at last, after a couple of second-place finishes, in 1941.

play, of course, and the management held off taking any paying customers, but the producer had to pay a few extra green fees to keep the course clear. In conclusion, Nicklaus came from one shot behind after nine holes to birdie the 18th and win by a stroke.

Arnold Palmer played Julius Boros on the island of Eleuthera, in the Bahamas, for the 1968 series. Interestingly, Boros always considered Arnie one of his "pigeons," someone he could beat whenever they got close in competition. The deceivingly soft-spoken Boros would make the comment about Palmer being an easy mark with a sly smile. In truth, Boros did seem to have Arnold's number. He beat him (and Jackie Cupit) in a play-off for the 1963 U.S. Open, at The Country Club in Brookline, Mass. And in the 1968 PGA Championship, Boros made a beautiful pitch on the final hole to save par and defeat Arnie (and Bob Charles) by a stroke.

Eleuthera, in 1967 (when the match was filmed), was still a British protectorate. Hence, the rules of the Royal & Ancient Golf Club of St. Andrews (the R&A), were in effect and the players could use the smaller British ball that was still in the game. (It was 1.62 inches in diameter; the American was, and is, 1.68. A year later the British tour players decided to switch to the bigger ball for their circuit on the theory that it was harder to play, especially in the wind, and therefore would make them more competitive against the dominating Americans.) Palmer decided to play the bigger ball. Boros opted for the smaller ball to get a better reaction in the strong and steady wind blowing across the island. A shrewd move by a man who gave off an air of casual indifference. Beneath that exterior was, in fact, a boiling hot and smart competitor. Boros also had a masterful touch with everything from the driver to the wedge and putter, no matter the size of the ball.

From the first hole on, Boros was outdriving Palmer, which seemed contrary. Palmer was famous for his powerful, hit 'em hard golf, while Boros had by contrast a smooth, rhythmic swing. Swing easy, hit hard, was his credo. As the match progressed and Boros continued to outdrive Palmer, Arnie became conscious of his reputation and decided he better let his fans in on why. He asked George Rogers and Gene Sarazen to remind the audience that Boros was playing the smaller British ball, which gave more distance in any case, and especially into the wind. His request was honored, but Boros still got the best of his "pigeon."

For those with an egalitarian streak, the match between Ken Venturi and Jean Garaialde, in Versailles, France was telling and discouraging. The gallery, as one can imagine, was highly partisan, all the more in Charles de Gaulle's France. The sentiment for a Garaialde victory over the American was palpable. At one point in the round Venturi got into a rules dispute with the referee, a French woman. She was a quality amateur golfer, knew her stuff, and was not in the least intimidated by Venturi or the situation. In fact, she had right on her side and although Venturi argued forcefully, he lost. When he finally relented, a cheer went up from the gallery.

It was a close contest. The Frenchman was giving the celebrated, dramatic winner of the 1964 U.S. Open a good go, and the closer he got to victory the warmer the gallery's response was to him. Indeed, Garaialde did win out and immediately after, many in the gallery strutted with Gallic pride from the 18th into the clubhouse to have a celebratory drink. Alas, being a professional, Garaialde was not allowed in the clubhouse to share in that libation. The rules of the club forbade it.

In 1964, Tommy Jacobs played Chi Chi Rodriguez at the Lyford Cay Club in Nassau, and gave the colorful Puerto Rican a nice little drubbing. The weather was beautiful, the scenery grand on this posh redoubt for the rich and famous, but Jacobs was antsy to get out of town once the match ended. One would think he might spend a day or two relaxing in this lap of luxury. It became clear a few days later why he was so anxious to hit the road. He was "feeling it," as they say about athletes who have found a good rhythm and touch, a heightened competitive energy. At the U.S. Open the following week, at the Congressional CC in Washington, D.C., Jacobs fired a second round 64, which equaled the lowest score ever recorded in the national championship. With it he took the 36-hole lead, and kept it through 54 holes. He fell to a 76 on the final day, though, as Ken Ven-

Tommy Jacobs, right, Sarazen, and Chen Ching-Po having a chat in between shots during the match played in Hong Kong in 1962. Two years later Jacobs played Chi Chi Rodriguez, in Nassau, the Bahamas. Here they are having fun during an interview with Sarazen. A week later, in the U.S. Open played in steamy Washington, D.C., Jacobs, perhaps having grown accustomed to playing in hot weather while in Nassau, shot a blistering 64 in the second round at the Congressional Golf Club to take the lead. He eventually finished second to Ken Venturi.

turi shot his superb 70 while on the verge of collapsing from the intense heat. Jacobs finished second by four to Venturi, but had a fine championship that those involved in the Shell show liked to believe, quietly, diplomatically, was the result of his warm-up (*sic*) against Chi Chi in Nassau.

One of the best-played matches of the entire series was in Greece between Tony Lema and Roberto DeVicenzo. Both golfers exuded a charming personality, each in their own way. DeVicenzo displayed as usual a good-natured warmth of being, completing the equation with his quaint distortions of the English language. And of course he played excellent golf. Lema was one of the most brilliant golfers to come down the line in many years. He had a long, flowing, leggy swing and a coy smile that twinkled with the aura of someone thoroughly enjoying his time on the planet. Lema was one of the few golfers who appeared on the Shell show to stay over in Europe for a few days to take in the sights, the food, and the Continental lifestyle.

In Greece, Lema and DeVicenzo combined their naturally attractive personae with a close and extremely well-played match on the painted fairways of the Glyfada Golf Course. Lema defeated DeVicenzo, 66 to 67. The golf was all the better for the fact that they played on a course that was not in the best condition. Raphael's paint job on the fairways was, after all, only a cosmetic treatment.

After the second year of the program, it was decided by someone in Shell's hierarchy that it would be a good idea to include a match between women. There may have been a push for this by a feminist group, but if so it was on the quiet. In any case, in 1964 the great Mickey Wright played Brigitte Varangot in Portugal. The next year, there were two women's matches — Barbara Romack vs. Isa Goldschmid in Monte Carlo, and Marley Spearman vs. Marilynn Smith in Luxembourg. Smith appeared again, in 1966, to play the diminutive Canadian amateur Marlene Streit in Norway. Streit played again, in Toronto, against Wright. Finally, in the next to last series U.S. Women's Open champion and future LPGA Hall of Famer Carol Mann played Sandra Haynie in Switzerland. That was followed in the last series by Haynie,

Sarazen watches closely the graceful, fluid swing of Tony Lema, who played a match in Denmark in 1964 against Carl Poulsen. Lema, the British Open champion in 1964, was a very popular player who appeared on two Shell shows before his untimely death in a small-plane crash in 1965.

In Estoril, Portugal, Sarazen discusses strategy with Mickey Wright (right) and her opponent in the match held there in 1963, Brigitte Varangot.

Mickey Wright watches the result of a drive during her match in Portugal, in 1963, against Brigitte Varangot. George Rogers, at back of tee, also watches...and narrates.

Mann, and Kathy Whitworth playing (in the revised format, to be outlined later), in Thailand.

The Shell match that has been the most storied, and sought-after in video, is the one between Sam Snead and Ben Hogan at the Houston Country Club in Houston, Texas. Only after Hogan passed away was Shell able to distribute the video. Apparently, Hogan forbade it in his deal with Shell. He was famous for protecting his image, and was not wont to give it away for free.

The match has become part of American golf legend. The sentiment, though, is not something that has been nurtured by nostalgists. It was a super attraction when it was played in June 1964 (it aired in 1965). There was no problem getting enough people to camouflage the cameras. There were times when the cameramen had a difficult time breaking through the throng to set up in their positions. The estimated live gallery was close to 10,000; a huge turnout, by far the biggest live audience in the history of the program. For good reason. Snead and Hogan were the titans of the game for an entire generation beginning in the late 1930s. (Byron Nelson was in the same category until he retired from competitive golf, for the most part, in 1946. Snead would carry on as a senior tour player into the 1980s.)

They were celebrated figures in the game by dint of personality, as well as their superb talent for golf. Snead was the colorful "country boy" in a dapper straw hat who had the most lissome, fluid golf swing the game had ever seen. Hogan, wearing his simple white cap and gray and white clothes, had a golf swing often likened to a machine operating on a production line; a very fast, but very precise machine. He was a stoical man on the surface, his lips shut tightly on an ever-present cigarette, the look in his eyes burning with intensity. Snead was the supreme natural athlete, gifted with rhythm and power. Hogan was cerebral in his approach to the game. Hogan, though, brought another dimension to the party. He represented courage as few athletes ever have or will. He had suffered extraordinary physical hurt when, in early 1949, his car was struck head-on by a speeding bus on a highway in Texas. Many thought he would not live through it, and everyone thought he would never play golf again. Except Hogan. In less than a year he returned to competitive golf, and in his first tournament after recuperating lost in a play-off for the Los Angeles Open to Sam Snead. That by itself was an incredible performance. He went one, make that ten, better later that year. In the U.S. Open at Merion in June 1950, Hogan won a three-way play-off against George Fazio and Lloyd Mangrum that sealed his greatness for all time.

The Snead-Hogan rivalry was as natural as the balata in the golf balls they used. What made this match all the more intriguing was the fact that Hogan deigned to be there in the first place. After nearly winning his fifth U.S. Open, at age 48—the 1960 at the Cherry Hills

CC in Denver, where Arnold Palmer won in dramatic fashion—Hogan began a self-imposed reclusiveness that marked the last third of his life. Whenever he was asked to play in a tournament, or give a special exhibition, he said he wouldn't because his game was not fit for public display. But here he was, the proud champion coming out to play his archrival, who had not come close to quitting the competitive scene and was still playing outstanding golf. Snead won his last tournament on the PGA Tour, the 1965 Greater Greensboro Open, at the age of 53. He continued to play well in subsequent years, and was a bulwark in the growth of the Senior PGA (now Champions) Tour.

Why did Hogan come out for this one? For one thing, he was doing his friend, Freddie Corcoran, a favor (just as he did when he entered the 1971 Westchester Classic, which Corcoran was hired to promote). And, as noted earlier, because he was anxious to promote his golf equipment company, which was only a few years old and struggling. Finally, as also noted earlier, he demanded and received a $25,000 appearance fee. So, Hogan wasn't quite the proud purist he would lead you to believe, but never mind. He was out there, and he gave good value—one of the finest rounds of golf from tee to green anyone had ever seen. Not only that, he even contributed a 45-second golf tip at the end of the show. Hogan talking golf swing was rare to hear and see, and on the Shell show people discovered how articulate the man famous for his tight-lipped manner could be on the subject he knew best.

Hogan arrived a day or so before the match, and pointedly eschewed the public relations opportunities staring him in the face. He said not a word to anyone as he walked directly into the pro shop every day to pick up his playing partner for the day, the head pro. It was only with him that he played his practice rounds. Snead did not join him. And by all means, no Shell executives or the company's best customers were going to tee it up with Mister Ben Hogan, thank you.

Truth to tell, Snead could be every bit as difficult, but he had a way about him that made him seem more approachable. He was a wonderful storyteller, although the more laughs he got the more he would lower the level of the humor until it got to raunchy bathroom tales. Hogan was a very proper, polite man except when crossed or being asked to do something he didn't want to do.

The Houston Country Club course was designed by Robert Trent Jones Sr., as were many of the courses played in the series. It was relatively new, and typical of Jones's work at the time—long, straight-away runway tees, huge bunkers, enormous greens. Hogan was not enamored of Jones's designs. Ten years earlier he won the U.S. Open at an Oakland Hills CC layout, in Detroit, that Jones had reworked into what Hogan reportedly called a "monster." Hogan relished the story he was told about the Houston CC layout, that Jones forgot to build one hole. When the discrepancy was discovered Jones came back to complete the job, but now had little room to work with. The best he could do was squeeze in a horseshoe par-5 in which the green was about 100 yards directly opposite the tee from which the hole began. Upon hearing the story, Hogan said, in his best sardonic style, "Anyone can hang out a shingle that says golf architect."

Having prepared himself for the long waits between shots, Hogan was patient and uncomplaining as the match progressed. He even went so far as to make a joke, sort of. The writer on the show was relaying to Rogers and Sarazen the clubs the golfers were playing to the greens, and on one hole where it was obvious he would hit a wedge, the writer said, "Wedge, Mr. Hogan?" "No, an Equalizer." That was the name of the wedge in his company's club line, and he was trying for a bit of a plug. He actually cracked a slight smile when he said Equalizer. Ben Hogan, in competition, showing some levity. It was quite a surprise. He got the plug.

Hogan's golf from tee to green was absolutely perfect. His swing, tightly wound as the club moved around his body on a flat plane, always gave the impression that he could not possibly be off line. And on this day he never was. It was a magnificent display of ball control from tee to green. He didn't miss a fairway from the tee, hit every green in regulation except for the par-5 third hole, which he hit in two. That came after he drove off the tee and play was suspended due to a fearsome lightning and thunderstorm. Hogan marked his ball in the fairway and didn't return to it for about three hours. When play resumed he nailed a 4-wood from a slightly sidehill lie onto the green. True, he got to hit a few warm-up shots before returning to play, but it was nonetheless a remarkable display of self- and swing-control.

On the greens Hogan was something else. Where he was entirely sure of himself playing drivers and irons, at putting he was almost catatonic. He stood over his putts seemingly forever before finally starting his stroke. People in the gallery were whispering, "C'mon Ben, get it back," and, "Damn, the man can't get that blade to move." It was painful to watch this nonpareil golfer having to struggle so with the putter. It wasn't all bad, of course. When he finally did get the putter to move the stroke was a kind of jerk/thrust. But he only three-putted once, and made three nice putts for birdies (and one two-putt for a fourth), to score a three under par 69.

Snead never had the ball control of Hogan, especially with the driver, which may be one reason why Sam never won the U.S. Open and Hogan won four. However, in the Shell match Sam didn't drive poorly at all. In at least two instances he outdrove Hogan by 25 yards. Sam only missed two greens in regulation, and had two putts lip out that if they fell would have made a significant difference in the outcome. In short, Snead played quite well. But his golf was overshadowed by Hogan's ultra-brilliant shotmaking, not to say the unusual force of his personality, his storied personal history, and the fact that he was playing before a home-state crowd. All came together to give the ambiance a distinctly Hogan-favored flavor.

Sam was very much attuned to the Hogan aura that permeated the scene, and by way of countering tried a few bravado shots. Nothing really rambunctious, except perhaps for a driver off the fairway on the back nine. He didn't catch it, but it didn't hurt him. He three-putted the last green when it didn't matter anymore, and shot a one-over par 73. It was the first time in four head-to-head contests that Hogan beat Sam. The three that Sam won were in true competition,

REGLAS LOCALES

1. · El juego se regirá por las reglas adoptadas
por la U. S. G. A., excepto cuando sean mo-
dificadas por una regla local.

2. · Se considerará "Out Of Bounds" las cercas,
estacas blancas, canales de concreto, cami-
nos, con excepción del canal que atraviesa
el hoyo 5 que es considerado obstáculo de
agua.

TARJETA PROVISIONAL

one a play-off for the 1954 Masters, a fact of which Sam was always very proud.

The Hogan-Snead match was the first to be filmed for the 1965 series (it was the sixth to be aired), and was directed by Lee Sholem, who had been hired when Dick Darley left the production. Sholem was a Hollywood director who played the part in the classic 1930s tradition—ascot, beret, lots of hand-waving, and in a rather loud voice magnified all the more by his use of a megaphone. His history was making small, low-budget B-movies; his reputation was for making them quickly. No extra takes unless absolutely necessary, setups done with a minimum of fuss, thereby keeping production costs within budget and sometimes below. Hence his nickname in the trade, "Roll 'em" Sholem. Alas, golf is not a fast game by its nature, and filming it for *Shell's Wonderful World of Golf* slowed the process even more, what with all those cameras in the pre-Charlie Okun period to get set up for every shot played. Sholem had no experience with golf, one way or another, and here he was thrown to the lions, so to speak. He not only had to deal with a game he knew little about, but with two outsized stars and a very large live audience that had little to no knowledge of what it took to make a television program.

For all that, Sholem did a decent job of it. Until he got to the last hole. He wanted to arrange it so Hogan and Snead would hit their second shots, putt out, then walk directly into the closing interview with Sarazen and Rogers—all in one fell swoop. It took some thought on where to place the cameras so they could film the long sequence seamlessly, if only because he couldn't be sure where they would hit their second shots, what angles they would be putting from, and so forth. It took much more time than anyone expected, including Hogan. Close to 20 minutes were consumed as Sholem ordered cameras here and there, rescinding them for new ones, all in the style of C.B. DeMille doing *Cleopatra.* The 1960s Texas gallery, in its best conservative dress for the occasion, became not so much restless as satirical. Chuckles and joke lines ran through the crowd, and there were nervous glances at Hogan, who was working on a third cigarette while waiting to play his final shot. At last, all was set. Sholem then shouted, "Your shot, Mr. Hogan. Take your time." It was the "take your time" that did Sholem in. A huge roar of laughter rose up out of the crowd, and once the show was in the can, so was Sholem. He did not fit the Shell Company image, and Fred Raphael took over as director for the remainder of the series.

In the eighth year of the series there was a format change. With so much more golf appearing on television, the Shell show did not have anywhere near the exclusivity it once enjoyed. The new people at Shell who inherited the project when Spaght and Biggar retired felt a change in the competitive format would give it a little more zing in the ratings. A rise in prize money was another hopeful incentive to attract viewers. The format devised was an elimination tournament between men players (one three-way match was played by women—Carol Mann, Kathy Whitworth, and Sandra Haynie that was not part of the men's event.) There were six preliminary matches at stroke-play, with three players in each. The winners went to the semifinals, and the two winners in the semis played in the final. It was a 10-show series, including the women's contest. The winner won a total of $37,000 ($7,000 in the preliminary round, $10,000 in the semifinal, $20,000 in the final). It did not fare well.

Until 1958, the PGA Championship had always been played at match play. This format was abandoned in 1958, in large part, or perhaps wholly out of a concern that the final would be between players not well enough known by the general public to be good draws at the

Among the celebrity referees for the matches was Francis Ouimet, seen here with Sarazen at The Country Club in 1965, where and when Billy Casper played Doug Sanders. It was at The Country Club, in 1913, when Ouimet, a young amateur with only a local reputation, astonished the golfing world by defeating the great British professionals Harry Vardon and Ted Ray in a play-off for the U.S. Open championship.

"box-office." As television coverage of golf increased, as well as that of sports such as baseball and football that always had a wider audience, it was felt the PGA Championship had to get more into the show business. In 1950, for example, Chandler Harper met Henry Williams Jr. in the final. In 1953, Walter Burkemo played Felice Torza to decide the championship. These were not star-studded contests, to say the least, for the finals of a major title. Television ratings were not very good for these affairs. In a few instances a star played, but not against another one. Sam Snead playing Johnny Palmer, and Ben Hogan up against Mike Turnesa just didn't ring of bullion. Indeed, money was becoming an important issue now that television was beaming so much sports over the air. Ratings were driving the economics, and to get good ratings you needed stars up front, as many as possible. With that in mind the PGA Championship was switched over to a stroke-play competition so it could be reasonably assured that marquee players were at least in the field on Saturday and Sunday. Even if they weren't serious contenders, they could be shown.

The Shell show went against this new grain with its changed format, and was more or less predictably disappointed with the results. In its first year, 1969, the field began with some notable players—Billy Casper, Lee Trevino, Arnold Palmer, Chi Chi Rodriquez, Doug Sanders, and Julius Boros—but the final was between Frank Beard and Ben Arda. Beard was a well-regarded American touring pro, a leading money winner but never the winner of a major title, and prosaic in his approach to the game. Arda was a pleasant little man from the Philippines, no bigger than a jockey, who did not hit the ball with great authority. What's more, he rarely if ever played in the United States and was effectively an unknown with a record of overall achievement so slim even the cleverest, most creative publicity man could not draw an audience's eye.

Little wonder that for the next year's series, only seven shows were produced. This time only men professionals played. Ben Arda was not asked back to defend his title, and in the final, at the Olympic Golf Club, in San Francisco, dour, stoop-shouldered Dan Sikes played the popular but foreign DeVicenzo. Sarazen didn't even travel to the first six matches. He appeared on location only for the final match.

And so the Shell show went out more or less with a whimper. But its last breath was not a true measure of the pleasure it gave and its long-term impact on golf, and golf on television. Its overall effect was historic. It touched a lot of bases, if we can mix our sports metaphors.

The historical timing of the Shell show was such that viewers were able to see the evolution in golf swing technique that was occurring in the game. There was a significant generational shift in golf technique that began in the 1960s, especially among European, and specifically British players that was mirrored in the series. In Bernard Hunt, Dai Rees, and Eric Brown, for example, we saw the flat, wristy swing that was the trademark of British golfers up until that time. It was a swing developed in large part to contend with the windy conditions in which they played so much of their golf. The changeover was first noticed in Tony Jacklin, who played in the penultimate Shell show series.

Jacklin was in the forefront of modern British golfers, more enterprising, less stuck in the old ways. He made a point of playing an entire year on the U.S. PGA Tour to gain some insight on the techniques being developed by the best players in the world, and to feed on the high level of competition they offered, week after week. He learned valuable lessons, for in 1970 Jacklin became the first Briton to win the U.S. Open in 50 years. Jacklin's swing resonated his American experience—it was not as hand-oriented, and had a more upright plane. The fullest expression of that process would be Nick Faldo, a decade later.

Although this is considered mainly in retrospect, viewers of the Shell show then and especially now could (and can, via videos of the programs available through the Shell Oil Company's public relations department) see how idiosyncratic or individualistic were the swings of American professionals who came of age in the 1940s and 1950s.

Sarazen checks out a near-make by Chen Ching-Po in his match against Tony Lema in Japan. The Japanese caddies, all women, covered up against the sun.

In those days, before video cameras and the remarkable proliferation of swing technique information through books, magazines, and more and better informed teachers, everyone made up a swing on their own. There was Miller Barber flying his right elbow; Gay Brewer twirling the club on his backswing like a conductor's baton; Billy Casper sliding his right foot down the line in his follow-through; slump-shouldered Bob Rosburg (and Casper) putting brilliantly with a short, jabby stroke developed for the slower greens of the time; Doug Sanders with a swing short enough to complete in a phone booth; Tony Lema coiling his body like a piece of silver foil. Swing aficionados can have a wonderfully informative time watching the entire series with only swing technique in mind.

For another thing, people who watch the series now, some 40 years after they were filmed, are amazed at how slow the greens appeared to be. By today's standards, they most certainly were. Even today's public fee golfers play on faster and smoother putting surfaces. The advances in turf technology over the past four decades have been enormous, and have changed the nature of the game. Putting is not as chancy as it was; the greens are more uniform as to speed and texture. The advent of "soft-spikes" has made them even more reliable.

Naturally, everyone involved in the production of the *Shell's Wonderful World of Golf* series knew who won the matches well before they appeared on television. Ever cautious of its image, the Shell Company tried to keep these results secret to prevent gamblers from taking advantage of advance notice. Hal Power remembers that every year after the matches were played Gordon Biggar hid the results of all the matches in a still undisclosed location. No one at Shell, K&E, or on Fred Raphael's production staff was sworn to secrecy, but there were very few known instances when anyone tried to make a killing betting on the outcome of the matches. Indeed, in one of them it was quite the opposite.

Fred Raphael told the story of being in his favorite New York City bar one Sunday late afternoon in winter watching the Snead-Nicklaus match at Pebble Beach. Some people at the bar were betting the bartender on the hole-by-hole outcome, and the match. Either they were lucky, or had some inside information, but one way or the other they took the barkeep for a good piece of change. After everyone left, Raphael told the bartender he could get even next week by betting Gerry DeWit would beat Byron Nelson, in the match in Holland. He also told the bartender that Nelson would shoot an 80. The bartender didn't believe him; Byron Nelson shooting 80! Fuhgeddaboudit. The next Sunday, Raphael saw the bartender betting on Nelson all the way, and once again losing his shirt. When Nelson hit his drive out-of-bounds on the last hole, and shot 80, the bartender paid off and then asked Raphael what he knew about the program. Raphael told him he was the producer. The bartender got very excited at that, and wanted to know the results of the next week's match between Phil Rodgers vs. Frank Phillips, in Singapore. Raphael said, "You had your chance last week. Sorry, pal."

Raphael's nephew, Dick Ashe, who worked as a production manager on the show, had a different story on the same tack. Ashe hung out at a bar in his hometown of Secaucus, New Jersey. The owner of the joint knew of Ashe's connection with the Shell show, and asked him who won the match coming up between Tony Lema and Roberto DeVicenzo in Greece. For obvious reasons. Ashe was good at his work on the show, but wasn't much into golf. He thought DeVicenzo won, and said so. He got it wrong. He didn't go back to that bar again.

Some of the people who worked on the Shell show went on to do interesting and productive work in golf, and otherwise. The coauthor of this book (Al Barkow) became the editor-in-chief of *Golf* and *Golf Illustrated* magazines; has written a number of books on the history of American golf; and instructional books in collaboration with a number of professionals; and appeared on television for over 10 years doing commentaries for "Inside the PGA Tour" and the "Senior PGA Tour" shows.

Herbert Warren Wind went on to make an even deeper imprint on golf literature with his journalistic essays on the major golf championships for the *New Yorker* magazine. As we speak, Herb is in retirement in Massachusetts.

Charlie Okun made the jump to Hollywood motion pictures, and over the years has been the producer of numerous outstanding feature films, including *The Accidental Tourist, Grand Canyon, Wyatt Earp, Silverado,* and *I Love You to Death.*

Edna Forde lives in Ireland, and works occasionally on film projects.

Dick Darley retired from filmmaking and is living in Sedona, Arizona.

Gene Sarazen passed away in his 97th year. He had finally slowed up a little physically, but was sharp of mind to the very end of his days.

Jimmy Demaret more or less retired to run his Champions Golf Club in Houston, Texas with his partner, Jackie Burke Jr. He passed away in 1986 but before that was instrumental in the development of the Senior PGA Tour (now the Champions Tour), as we shall see in a moment.

Hal Power retired from the Shell Company, and lives, suitably enough, at Demaret's (and Jackie Burke's) Champions Golf Club. Hal was an important source of information for this book.

Fred Raphael passed away at the age of 80, in 2000, but before that he made a huge contribution to golf with his conception of a made-for-television golf tournament called The Legends of Golf. After the Shell show closed down, Fred went into a kind of semiretirement. He had to more or less catch his breath after the long and often arduous nine-year marathon he had been on.

In the early 1970s Raphael was ready to get active again, and with an idea he had conjured up 10 years earlier. He caught the tenor of the times. The country was in a nostalgic mood. Old-Timer days were becoming a staple of major league baseball, with celebrations of re-tired players regularly staged in every ballpark in the country. Raphael felt something on this order would captivate older golf fans. The germ of the idea, and its very title came to him in 1963. He was having lunch with Gene Sarazen during that year's Masters tournament. Sarazen was still competing in the event, and had scored 147 for 36 holes. That put him in a tie with none other than Arnold Palmer, who was in his prime as a championship golfer. This is indicative, of course, of how much of a golfer Sarazen was. He was 61 years old at the time.

At lunch after the second round of play, Raphael asked Gene who he was paired with the next day. Sarazen said, "Tomorrow an old leg-end and a new one will tee it up." It was the word legend that jumped out at Raphael. It bespoke his basic germinating concept and the title for it.

In 1963, Raphael had his plate full producing *Shell's Wonderful World of Golf,* and was not in a position to do anything else. The time wasn't quite right anyway. When it was, he acted. With Jimmy Demaret helping him formulate the concept, Raphael put together a tournament for professional golfers 50 years old or older who had won major titles and/or other important championships in their careers; legends of the game. They would be paired and compete in a best-ball stroke-play competition that would appear on network television.

In 1978, the first Legends of Golf tournament was played on the Onion Creek CC course in Austin, Texas. (It would host the first 12.) Jimmy Demaret designed the course, and had a heavy interest in the real estate development with which it was attached. It wasn't a great layout, but none of the contestants invited to play minded at all. With this opportunity to get back into competition, and especially tilt for a total purse of $400,000, old pros who thought the good times were long past would have played on a parking lot. The winners would get $50,000 each, the last-place finishers $10,000 each. When two-time PGA champion Paul Runyan was invited to the Legends tournament he told Demaret, "Do you realize I can finish last and win more money than I ever won in any tournament I ever played in?" Runyan, by the way, was the first official leading money winner on the PGA Tour when in 1934 he won a total of $6,767.

The opener also featured such legends as Demaret, Tommy Bolt, Julius Boros, Roberto DeVicenzo, Sam Snead, "Lighthorse" Harry Cooper, Cary Middlecoff, Peter Thomson, and Kel Nagle. All had won at least one major title, in many cases more than a few. Ben Hogan was invited for the first tournament and for many others in subsequent years, but refused each time. The first Legends of Golf tournament was won by the team of Sam Snead and Gardner Dickinson. It was a good show. Sam, at 66, was a marvel of athleticism with his still long and smooth swing. He made six birdies in the final round. The ratings were sufficient to bring the show back the following year, and that was when it and senior golf took off.

In the 1979 Legends of Golf tournament, Tommy Bolt and Art Wall Jr. were in a play-off with Roberto DeVicenzo and Julius Boros that was not only a display of excellent and highly competitive golf, but an evocation of hearty, warm-spirited compassion that was missing from the deadly serious young men playing on the PGA Tour.

Bolt and DeVicenzo were the main players on this stage. They traded birdies for five holes with superb approach shots and dramatic putting. When the always animated Bolt holed an 18-footer on the fifth extra hole for a birdie three, he pointed a finger at DeVicenzo as if to say, "Take that, buddy!" DeVicenzo then holed a slightly shorter putt to keep the play-off alive, and after doing so returned the finger-pointing gesture. It was good golf and fun too. On the next hole DeVicenzo made the putt that brought him and Boros the victory, but by then the real winner was senior golf. The show got rave reviews. Journalists and television viewers were enthralled at how well these old-timers could still play, and what a wonderful vivacity they brought to it all. Raphael had been unable to find a sponsor for the first two years of the show, but after 1979 the Liberty Mutual Insurance Company came on and is still the sole sponsor of the event.

After the DeVicenzo-Bolt engagement and the national response to it, Gardner Dickinson, Dan Sikes, and other senior players, including Boros, Don January, Bob Goalby, and Snead, realized they might take this senior thing a little farther. They founded the Professional Golfers Association of Seniors with the intention of developing a tournament circuit for over-50 pros. They got television interested, which prompted PGA Tour commissioner Deane Beman to take it seriously, and the Senior PGA Tour was formed. The first tournament for the new circuit took place in June 1980 at the Atlantic City Country Club, which ironically enough, was owned by Leo Fraser, the pro who went out and hit those balls for the camera in the aftermath of the Nelson-Littler match at Pine Valley that broke ground for the *Shell's Wonderful World of Golf* series.

The renamed Champions PGA Tour has since become a hugely successful enterprise in which, in 2003, the total prize money for a 31-tournament circuit was over $52 million.

It may seem far-fetched, perhaps self-serving, but it can be said that if not for *Shell's Wonderful World of Golf,* the Senior PGA Tour may never have seen the light of day. There is a theory of history that says two ships colliding in midocean was an event fated to happen before the ships were ever built, the captains and their crews born, and so on. In the same vein, one could say that if Fred Raphael hadn't been given the job of producing *Shell's Wonderful World of Golf*, or his boss Marty Ransohoff decided not to take on the project in the first place, or Monte Spaght had a heart attack before signing off on the project, or any of hundreds if not thousands of small incidents seemingly inconsequential at the time hadn't occurred, there would be no Champions PGA Tour today. In a word, *Shell's Wonderful World of Golf* has left quite a legacy to the old Scotsgame.

HALMSTAD GOLFKLUBB

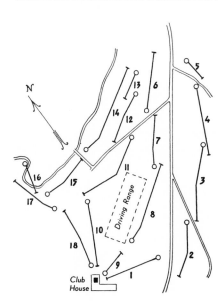

CHAPTER 4

LETTERS TO BOB

◆ ◆ ◆

Gene Sarazen began a regular correspondence with Bobby Jones in 1965, three years into his participation on the Shell show, writing from various locations around the world where he traveled with the production. He maintained the correspondence until 1970, when the show was terminated. Most of the letters follow, a few mildly edited for the sake of personal privacy. They reflect the warm feelings Sarazen had for the great amateur champion and cofounder of the Augusta National Golf Club and the Masters tournament. They were born in the same year, 1902, their wives were both named Mary, and of course they shared the highest rung as players in American and international championship golf.

The letters seem to have served a number of purposes. Sarazen wanted to entertain his old friend, who he knew was confined to a wheelchair and physically deteriorating from syringomyelia, a chronic progressively degenerative disease of the spinal cord. Jones's body was painfully shriveling as the disease took its dreadful toll, and Sarazen hoped his letters would perhaps help ease his agony a little. They did just that, according to Charles Elliott, a third cousin of Jones who helped him through the difficult last years of his life by taking him on fishing trips. Years after the fact Elliott wrote a letter to Sarazen describing how much Jones enjoyed the correspondence: "During that period," Elliott wrote, "you were writing to Bob every week or so, and from what he said your letters gave him every bit as much pleasure or perhaps even more than his fishing. You were one

*Sarazen and his good friend and letter-writing confidante Bobby Jones,
preparing for the conversation they had during the Julius Boros, Sam Snead
match at the Peachtree Country Club, in Atlanta, Georgia in 1966.*

of his most favorite friends, and he talked a lot about his long association with you....[Thank you] for giving Bob so many delightful
hours that helped him through those last years when he was suffer-
ing so much."

Sarazen also used the correspondence to unburden himself of
some of his frustrations with coannouncer George Rogers, when they
were the announcing team. In fact, Sarazen used Jones's influence to
help relieve that situation in Gene's favor. Jones put in a soft word or
two to the people at Shell. The letters also include some travel writing, if you will. And, they also were an outlet for some of Sarazen's
social and political views, not to say the state of modern golf course
architecture and the attitude of some modern-day professional golfers. Sarazen was nothing if not a man of opinions strongly felt. Jones
responded with letters to Sarazen, but his condition made it difficult
to keep up in volume. (Jones's letters to Sarazen were not available
for this book.)

Here are the letters from Gene to Bob, beginning in April 1965, a couple of years after Sarazen's travels with the Shell show began. They end in 1970, the last year of the program. You will notice that each letter begins with *Dear Bob.* Sarazen knew well that Jones never liked being called Bobby.

From Manila, the Philippines—April 30, 1965

Dear Bob:

Your letter of April 19 has just arrived here. I am sure you will get action from the top brass. They have changed the format somewhat. I do considerable talking on the green with Rogers. While I don't describe the shots, I do have a chance to talk more about what happened. But it's what happens when they get into the cutting room, where Rogers plays a very important role.

It was nice of you to take time to write the letter. I appreciate it very much. And I know one person who will like it more is Mary, because it just burns her up to hear Rogers describe a shot when he can't break 90. It's show business, and I am becoming a ham like the rest. But I will not use the word great on a shot until I firmly believe it is great.

We finished our show here today, and oh boy was it hot. The temperature was over 100. I know the Squire lost weight. The nicest place to be is in your room with a bottle of Old Rarity and ice.

I have seen a big change in this place. I was here two years ago, and they haven't cleaned up the bloodstains from the war.

The other night the president of the Shell Oil Company gave a cocktail party. All the top brass was present, from the ex-pres [of the Philippines] to the [American] ambassador, and who do you think was there with brass buttons: R.T. Jones. "Not Jr." He is out building a golf course. He had his son with him.

They were leaving the next day for Tokyo. I can't imagine any-one coming out here looking for jobs or doing them. So far away, and the climate is either too warm or raining all the time.

We did a show at the Valley Club. It's really a beautiful place, very modern. The greens were so huge that it was nothing but an approach putt contest. Bob, I am against big greens.

The crew is getting ready to leave for Malaysia. They are stopping at Saigon. I refuse to land in Saigon. [He did, though.] I want to be the master of my own execution, not some travel agent. So I am going to Hong Kong, stop at Bangkok, then on to Malaysia.

Dow Finsterwald has left for home. Somewhat disap-pointed. [He lost to Ben Arda.] You know the prize money is ten grand, with seven for first. In my time I'd go around the world for that much money. We leave for Malaysia tonight. Pause. I just got a call that they cannot clear me through to Singapore. I'll have to stay overnight in Bangkok. I'll be damn glad when I get to Spain. Well, it's Hong Kong, Bangkok, and Kuala Lumpur, and "away we go." Give my best to Mary [Jones]. Augusta was not the same without her down there.

Cheerio, Gene.

P.S. Just got a call from the embassy, American. They want me to give a talk in Rangoon, Burma. I said I was working for Shell not the State Department.

Gene.

From the Federal Hotel, Kuala Lumpur, Malaysia, May 5, 1965

Dear Bob

Here in the steaming jungle of Malaysia. I want to tell you it's hot. Only salvation is it rains every afternoon. My air-conditioned room is my palace. I played golf this morning with the Deputy Premier. 6:30 A.M. That's the time they play on account of the heat.

Quite a contrast from that dried-up Manila. Here everything is green. Flowers, etc. They cut their fairways twice a day. They are not good courses, very old-fashioned.

Charlie Sifford arrived with his wife. They routed him by way of Saigon. He said, "Mr. Gene, isn't there any other way to go home? I don't like that place. All those men with machine guns." That day there was a war 10 miles from the airport. I said, Charlie have them route you by way of Bangkok. Boy, he sure had a scare.

I am beginning to get homesick. One more week and we'll take the big hop. Air service is not so good here. You have go south to Singapore and then back north to Bangkok. About 16 hours by jet. Traveling like this you don't even like to unpack. Tomorrow I do my course montage and away we go with the match. Did you receive the booklet from Bangkok? A very interesting place. Hot, and full of temples. Well Bob, that's all for now. My best to Mary. Cheerio, Gene.

From the Athens Hilton, Athens, Greece, May 12, 1965

For about five days I've been in a country where no Americans are allowed. Burma. The pressure came from the State Department for me to stop off on a goodwill mission. At first I refused. Finally, both the Shell people and the State Department forced me into going. It was a rough trip. Hot as hell. I arrived in Rangoon around two a.m. Met by a crowd. Mind you, I was the first American golfer to play there.

When I woke up that morning, Jack Higgins, who is connected with the American Embassy, handed me a sheet of paper. Every hour of the day was scheduled. Played a few holes

on two courses, a four-ball match in the afternoon, a clinic after the match. I told Higgins I wouldn't work that hard for
Lyndon B. Johnson. Well, the day was completed, then the fes-
tivities, cocktail party, and dinner party. How I am still alive I
don't know. Did you ever feel like fighting with your host? Well,
I did. The next day, Sunday, a match between the Burma Open
champion and myself. Up at five a.m., breakfast, ready to leave
for the club at six. I arrived and 400 people were having breakfast at the club. To them this was a big event. Something they
had never seen before, an international match. O Boy was it
hot. Ninety-five with humidity around 75 at seven a.m. I
grabbed two clubs and had about 20 swings and said let's go.
They were so curious that I didn't practice. The course was
good, but in terrible shape. Greens you couldn't hole a two-
foot putt on. On one hole a huge snake circled around my ball
and the crowd backed up. The [army] boys rushed in and killed
it. It was a viper six feet long. The most deadly snake in the
world. They would point out different spots on the course to
keep away from. There is a nest of cobras. Lovely place.

The country is now under military control. The people
couldn't be nicer. It was the greatest experience I ever had.
Sunday night the American Ambassador gave a reception in
my honor. I had to stand in line with him, shaking hands with
over 300 people. I was deeply touched when he told me that
he never could get the military boys to attend other parties.
Finally, the last day I had to play another match with the military boys at their own course. General Ne Win didn't come
out. They say things are shaky in the country. When he does
play there is a whole army of men with machine guns watching
over him. So I am just as glad he didn't come, although he is a
golf bug.

We ran the Hogan-Snead match at the club, then followed
by the 1962 Masters. They loved them both.

I told the embassy to send you some photographs that were taken during my visit. Thought you might enjoy seeing what the rest of the world looks like.

I left that morning around two a.m. and believe it or not a crowd was down to see me off. I felt very happy about my mission. I was also damn glad when that 707 was up 30,000 feet heading for Beirut. You can imagine what a change. The temperature here is around 55-60. Gee, I'm in a writing mood today. The weather is just beautiful. I haven't had a chance to see the place. We film here next week with Lema and DeVicenzo. It's five p.m. here but two a.m. in Burma. Sure been giving those sleeping pills a workout. It's hard as hell to catch up on sleep.

This is a beautiful hotel. The tourists come in army cots. The lobby is Forty Second Street at Fifth Avenue.

Well, Bob, I am running out of steam. I hope you enjoy my description of my trip to Burma. I'll tell you more about it in person at the Masters dinner next year. Next stop, Campo de Golf, Madrid, Spain.

From Athens, Greece, May, 13, 1965

Dear Bob

This is a beautiful place. I have fallen in love with Athens. My love to Mary, Gene.

From the Castellana Hilton, Madrid, Spain, May 23, 1965

Dear Bob

Arrived here from Greece. Had a nice smooth flight. Was just a little bit jittery since the night before, the same type of jet crashed just below, in Cairo. I have never seen a more beautiful country club anywhere in the world. Twenty-seven beautiful holes, wonderful turf, polo field, practice course that would make any of ours look terrible, school for caddies. It's a huge place, only 20 minutes from the center of the city. They have 12,000 members but only 800 play golf. I don't think anyone will break 70 in this match. Bobby Nichols against Ramon Sota.

The weather is dry and the course is in perfect shape. Plenty of watering. I just can't imagine the course having a long life. It borders on the college and property is scarce. Madrid is at its peak this time of year. Flowers all over the place, and the tourists are tying up traffic. Rooms are scarce. If you want a double room you better be two or they will give you a small closet for a single.

The movie crowd are all off to the see the bullfight. I told them that I'd seen my farmer fight a bull with a pitchfork. That's enough for me. Bob, did you receive the photographs from Burma? The embassy wanted to know if I wanted anyone to have some so I gave them your address. Think of me having a turkish bath when you see them.

Gene.

From the Castellana Hilton, Madrid, Spain—May 26, 1965

Dear Bob

Glad to hear you've been enjoying my letters to you. This club is surely one of the best in the world. I always thought of Spain as bull-fighting country, but believe me I saw two golf clubs in this town that I don't see anything equal to. The facilities—polo, tennis, swimming, soccer, playground for member's children, a school for caddies. And a church for caddies.

Had lunch with the Marquis de Bolorgue today. He told me all about Franco. The Marquis was and still is one of his original backers. I asked him if Franco played golf. He said when Franco was in exile in the Canary Islands he was playing the ninth hole when word came to him to leave and lead the revolution. He has a short course around the palace. The Marquis wants me to come back in November and have a game with him. They have 40 courses in Spain, and they are out for the American tourist. I am sure they will get a lot of golfers, because they have beautiful courses. The language barrier is terrific. The operators don't speak English, hotels are overcrowded. Leave tomorrow for good old Scotland. Put away the silks and bring out the wool.

The climate here is just beautiful. Nice dry air, sun out every day, temperature around 70. I can see this becoming a real boom country for American tourists.

I have two cocktail parties, then a dinner party at 11:00. I am going to leave a tag where to ship my body. My best to Mary and away we go to bonny Scotland.

Gene.

From the Turnberry Hotel, Ayrshire, Scotland, May 30, 1965

Dear Bob

This place should have some pleasant memories for you. It's just below Prestwick, and I know you have either played here or visited. Anyway, it's one of the finest seaside courses I have ever seen. There isn't anything that comes even close to it. The No. 9 is without a doubt the greatest par-4 hole I have ever seen. It's something like the 16th at Cypress Point, near Pebble Beach, only it's about 475. It's called Bruce's Castle. I am sorry that Snead or Hogan are not playing here. Dave Marr is playing an unknown by the name of George Will. They will surprise me if either shoots better than seventy five.

Today is Sunday. O, by the way, speaking of Old Rarity, coming up from London I sat next to a gentleman and we both had a few scotches. So I said, you know I have tried all over the world to buy Old Rarity whiskey, and no one carries it. I hope I am lucky enough to be able to purchase some in Scotland. He looked at me and said, Mr. Sarazen, I am a director of Bullock Lade Co., makers of Old Rarity. I'll see that you have a good supply. Well, the net result is my dresser is decorated with Old Rarity. I'll have to invite some of the boys up here to drink it up. This could only happen in Scotland.

Dave Marr just arrived. Looked very sleepy. Well Bob, the next letter will come from Oslo. Then away we go home. My best to Mary, Gene.

From the Turnberry Hotel Ayrshire, Scotland, June 1, 1965

Dear Bob

The pictures you were to receive from Burma were mailed to the wrong Jones. I received a letter from Trent Jones that they were sent to him from Augusta. Somebody goofed. I wrote Mrs. Trent that they were intended for you. I thought you might enjoy seeing what Burma golf is like.

Best to you, Gene.

From the Grand Hotel, Oslo, Norway, June 8, 1965

Here we are in the cold north. The apple blossoms are just coming out. Yesterday I was beginning to think I should get out my Hong Kong silk suits. Today it's cold, raining. Need Scotch woolen socks. You can't tell, we might be filming a ski match. This is our last show. Everybody is excited about going home. Our crew comes from all over the world—Australia, Manila, California. What a job to get tickets and reservations in order.

The course here is not too bad. It's used for skiing all winter. Only a short time ago they had six feet of snow, and the lake had 48 inches of ice. The greens are winterkill. We are looking all over for some green dye. Maybe with this rain more grass may come through.

I sure enjoyed my visit to Turnberry. My last day there I played golf with Stanley Morrison, captain of the club and owner of a distillery, scotch whiskey. That night he had his boy deliver a bottle of scotch, 35 years old. I am not drinking it, just sniffing it. It's too good to drink. Glen Grant.

Boy, I am anxious to get home. I talked to Mary last night. Perfect connection. She said never again. I've heard that before. Oh, the farm will look like heaven for a few weeks.

Bob, it's been great writing you from all around the world. If you had as much pleasure receiving them, then I feel good. Hope I didn't bore you with some of the petty things that go on.

My best to Mary. Haste ye back. Gene.

From Germantown, New York, June 24, 1965

Dear Bob

Thanks for yours of June 16th. Also, thanks for the clipping. It is one I could use in the book. I miss men like Grantland Rice. This present crop is not my cup of tea.

I remember so well in 1932 with you and Fred Newton having lunch and yours truly drinking beer. Everybody was burning the damn course up; and then all hell broke loose—two on the ninth. Will I ever forget that putt that started the fire—32-34. Read the papers today. You would think we didn't know how to play golf in those days. [Reference is to the third round of the 1932 U.S. Open, at Fresh Meadow CC, Flushing, NY, when Sarazen came to the par-3 ninth hole seven shots off the lead. He birdied the ninth to go out in 38, but came back in 32 for a 70 that left him only one shot off the lead. He played the final 18 that afternoon in 66, the lowest round in the championship's history to that date, and won by three strokes.]

I've been following the [U.S.] Open. Gary Player looks terrible swinging that club. Yesterday he missed three straight shots and made three pars. I do not like Trent Jones's architecture. Huge greens. That's why the 4-wood players with a good approach were scoring this year. They were talking about rough grass. According to TV the rough was almost like a fairway. I am very anxious to build a course with this Desmond Muirhead. He agrees with most of my ideas.

I received a letter from Cliff Roberts about making suggestions on the Augusta National. The one main suggestion is bringing your woods into play. Take for instance your second hole. The trap in the middle catches your members. Eliminate those and put a real one in 260 yards on the right. That would certainly force them to hug the left side. [This was done.] Rough grass is no test of golf. And I do not like tees 100 yards long. Short holes should have three different angles.

Where are you going for the summer? If you should be going to Pittsfield let me know. I'll drive up to see you. This is Sunday and Father's Day. My Mary is in church. That's where all good Marys should be.

Gene.

From Germantown, NY, July 26, 1965

Just a line to let you know how much I enjoyed the *Golf* magazine issue honoring your Grand Slam. I think they did a wonderful job.

Just returned from a quick trip to Detroit and California. Getting many requests for remodeling courses. Great many need remodeling. Traps 50 yards from greens. One course in Ann Arbor, Michigan was designed by Donald Ross. The layout was good, but the bunkering outdated (Barton Hills CC).

The weather here continues to be nice, but too dry. A week ago we had three inches of rain, which saved our corn. We have 100 acres. The apples show good progress, but if we don't have rain the roots will start calling on the fruit for moisture.

What do you think, I am going to play in the Thunderbird tournament. [A PGA Tour event, at the Westchester CC, White Plains, NY.] I'll have to brush up on all the new rules these pros have changed. The marking of the ball on the greens, etc. I don't know if you saw my story on the [U.S.] Open championship. I criticized the tour itself. It was a bore on TV. Gary Player would pick up his ball three times on the green. You thought he was picking up the Hope diamond. If they are going to clean their ball they should only touch it one time. Large greens have taken something out of the game. It's all long putts.

Cheerio, Gene.

From Germantown, NY, August 1, 1965

Dear Bob

Just returned from playing the Thunderbird tournament. Had a terrible experience. I was seven over par for the first six holes. Couldn't imagine what the hell was the matter with me. Finally I got started and finished the last 30 holes in two under par—78-71. The course is old-fashioned. They haven't made a change in 40 years. They were driving some of the par-4s and playing short irons for their second shots on the par-5s. That's enough tour golf for me this year. Gene.

From Germantown, NY, April 23, 1966

Dear Bob

Well, by now you should be well rested after the ordeal of ties the Masters had. I was in Mexico City at the time. Gay [Brewer] will never have a better opportunity to win a Masters. [Reference is to the 1966 Masters, which featured a three-way play-off between Jack Nicklaus, Gay Brewer, and Tommy Jacobs, which Nicklaus won in an 18-hole play-off. Brewer won the 1967 Masters by one stroke, over Bobby Nichols.]

We have filmed two shows. Glad to leave Mexico City and Caracas. I caught the trots in Mexico. Through the ice again. Boy, do they hate Americans [in Caracas]. I'd like to know where our Washington diplomats go when they say we're loved by all. I was lucky that my exit papers were all in order for my departure. Jimmy's [Demaret] were not, and he had to go through a lot of trouble and a delay of 48 hours. So you can imagine how much he loved Caracas.

Both shows are a great improvement. Jimmy D is so nice to work with.

In the Caracas match we had a very exciting hole. Billy Casper sliced a ball out-of-bounds, hooked his drive into another fairway, then proceeded to hole out his fourth shot. Another good feature of this year, we are doing the shows in one day.

It's so nice to be home for a couple of days. It's 85 today, and all the trees are popping with blossoms. Tomorrow I leave for Bermuda. From there to Casablanca, Rome, Germany, Paris, Holland, Wales, Canada, and Peachtree [in Atlanta, GA.]

You sure had beautiful weather at Augusta this year. And it was so nice to see you and Mary. All I can say is, God willing I'll see you in June.

Gene.

From The Mid-Ocean Golf Club, Bermuda, April 26, 1966

Dear Bob

They tell me you played this course once. I can understand why you just loved it. Blind tee shots, blind traps, and lovely rolling terrain. I am crazy about hilly courses. They feel so good in my legs.

This sure is a beautiful island, second to none for sheer beauty. This is the place where a man with a million will get lost. Great army of tax dodgers. Don't blame them. I am just jealous. They pay no income tax here, property tax is very small. They are so well organized that when somebody wants to buy a home or a lot they give him a blood test, then a financial going over. Then they tell him to take it or leave it.

Tony Lema plays Peter Alliss. Should be a good match, and a beautiful show. The greens are not too good. They are so short of water. Last year they had to purchase $65,000 worth of water from Florida.

Jimmy hasn't arrived. No one knows where he is. I am pretty sure he will show up on some jet. After his experience in Caracas I don't blame him for disappearing.

See you in June,

Gene.

From Hotel Miramar, Mohammedia, Morocco, May 1966

Dear Bob

Here we are, ready to leave for Rome. Finished here yesterday with Tom Weiskopf and Robert DeVicenzo. Roberto played beautiful golf, but Tom not too good. [He] has a lot to learn.

The course was very dry. They don't have any watering system here, and rain is very scarce. The natives play very little golf. Mostly tourists, but not many Americans. French, Germans, visitors from northern Europe, where it's still winter. This does not have too much to offer for the Yankee.

Our gallery was mostly navy personnel from a nearby base, In order to give it native atmosphere, they had to hire 40 camel drivers. The trip over was very nice, but the time was too long for the Squire. Seven hours to Paris without sleep, two hours holdover, and three hours down to here. It takes two days to get adjusted. Jimmy keeps saying why didn't you warn me about this?

It sure is great to be working with Jimmy. So much fun. I think you will like the show this year. We are calling the shots as we see them, and not covering up for anyone. I haven't heard who is going to play in Atlanta. They are trying to get Hogan-Snead, but Hogan is holding them up for big money. Palmer, Nicklaus, and Player are out. They have their own show. I am afraid pros are getting out of hand as far as money goes. They will have to stop somewhere or they will kill the business.

Fred Raphael, the producer of our show, tells me that we will finish Peachtree in seven hours. They are planning to have three camera crews. How sweet that sounds, although we have been finishing all our shows in far less than eight hours. Well, that's all from the globe traveler. Sure looking forward to seeing you at Peachtree and have some laughs.

Gene.

From the Paris Hilton, Paris, France, May 23, 1966

Dear Bob

Paris. What a beautiful city. Arrived from London. We had a good show at Porthcawl, Wales between Bob Rosburg and

Dave Thomas. Today I visited La Boulie Golf Course. The last time I played there was 1924, in the French Open. I did the first two rounds in 142. Then a Frenchman wanted to know how I was going to play my second shot on the first hole. I said I'll hook it around the—zee—trees. The hook never came off and I put four balls out-of-bounds. My third round was 89. When I went back to the hotel Mary asked how did I do. I said 89. O, that's wonderful [she said]. She thought a high score was good in golf. I told her I didn't go out to shoot pigeons. After 42 years the place was entirely different. Trees, O boy, they are huge. I never have seen so many beautiful flowers on any golf course. Every tee has a flower garden around it. We should have something unusual here. Venturi plays the French champion. [Jean Garaialde.] He played at Augusta.

This place is a madhouse. Nothing but confusion. This is by far the worst Hilton Hotel. I am afraid to send my suit to be pressed for fear I'll never get it back. It's by far the most expensive place I have ever seen. I am checking out tomorrow to a place closer to the course. It takes almost an hour by car, but when you arrive you're a nervous wreck. The Italian and French taxi drivers should be allowed to enter the Indianapolis race.

Everybody you talk to feels sorry for the DeGaulle action toward the U.S. They all say the same thing, that it won't be too long before we're together again.

Jimmy left me for a weekend in Texas. Between his phone bills and airplane tickets back and forth from Texas the Treasury Department isn't going to make much money on him.

Sam Snead has been signed up for the Atlanta match. I hope they will be able to get the Open champ to play him. [Gary Player.] Otherwise, I suggested Charlie Coe. Only two more after this and we will cross the old pond again for Toronto. Plane travel is very heavy. Before, it used to be only Americans traveled. Now, everybody is on the go. Well Bob, I started out to write a note and end up writing a book. See you soon, Gene.

From Germantown, NY, July 1, 1966

Dear Bob

Thank you for the letter. I talked to Mr. Biggar and you can rest assured that nothing will go on the air without your approval. [The reference is to the interview Jones did with Sarazen for the show in Atlanta, at the Peachtree CC.]

It was very nice of you to take time out for me. I want you to know how much I appreciated it. Besides, I enjoyed my visit with you.

I expect to be down your way soon. Had a game with a friend of yours at Greenville, S.C. Mr. Furman. Well, hope you are feeling better. It's been terribly hot here. Maybe I should spend my summer in Casablanca, where it's cooler.

The apple crop looks light, but healthy. Best to you, Gene.

From Germantown, Sept. 18, 1966

It seems ages since I last heard from you. How is the new book coming? Will Grimsley just came out with his new book. Sells for nineteen dollars and seventy five cents, a lot of money. I have one and it's worth it.

We've been having beautiful weather. The apples are coloring up well. Have a great crop, and your favorite red delicious is really big this year. Mostly due to a light crop. I went down to Washington last week. Played with Burmese General Ne Win. I have never seen anybody guarded so much. Every hole at Burning Tree was saturated with secret service men. The funny part of it was, they covered me every time I pulled out a club or went into the pocket of my bag for a ball. I was delighted when the game was over.

From the report I received on the Atlanta show, it was great. You will have a chance to see it some time in December. It goes on the air February 25. I'll be having a party in Atlanta on that day for the Martin-Marietta Co.

How is Mary? My Mary is fine, but I can't get her to stop smoking. I am leaving for Denver for a few days. Then, in the middle of October I am going to take Mary to Scotland for a week. She deserves a trip. Been here all summer.

Been watching some of the new shows [on television]. They are like new model cars. Very little change. Some of them better have a contract or they will go off the air. The live golf shows were very thrilling this year. The only dull one was the PGA, at Akron, Ohio. This will give you a laugh. I played in a sectional PGA event the other day. In Albany, NY. I shot a 69. The nearest player was six shots away. I used the cart.

Best always, Gene.

From Germantown, NY, Nov. 5, 1966

Dear Bob

I just returned from N.Y. The Atlanta show is great. You will like it very much. They did an excellent job in the cutting room. They will review it again, then Mr. Biggar is going to take it down and show it to you.

This is the time of year that show business gets exciting. Press parties, TV, appearances. I have about 10 stops, coast to coast to alert our viewers that we will be on the air again. I am enclosing our schedule. The Atlanta show goes on the air Feb. 25th. Good time. By then all the shows like the Hope Classic and Crosby Clambake will be back of us. I am sure you will enjoy the shows this year. Jimmy does a good job. A little too much talking on his part, but they intend to cut him back. As ever, Gene.

From Germantown, NY, January 9, 1967

Dear Bob

Thank you very much for the book and the nice things you had to say about the Squire. I haven't had a chance to read it through, but will. Demaret and myself just returned from a trip all over the USA promoting the show on radio, TV, newspapers. The only way I could create any excitement with the press was to suggest that TV is going to force the powers that be to increase the size of the hole, say a half inch. On TV a three-foot putt looks like six inches. The rank and file don't think much of a great player when they see him miss a three-foot putt on TV.

I was all set to leave for Atlanta for a private showing of the Peachtree show, but it was postponed. They will let you know when. I am leaving for Washington. They have a private showing for the Caracas match. This is for the ambassador of Venezuela. It will be a tough one, because we both disliked the place. They wouldn't let Jimmy out of the country. O well, this too shall pass. Best to you, Gene.

From Hotel Guatemala, Guatemala City, Guatemala, April 22, 1967

Dear Bob

Well, here we are again. Our first match was at St. Croix, a new course built by R.T. Jones. St. Croix was a nice island. The climate is very good. A very low humidity, more like Arizona. There's a terrible shortage of water, so dry. Liquor and perfume cheap and plenty. The big attraction at St. Croix is not the price of real estate, but taxes that are very little. Business can come to the island and not pay any taxes for 10 years. After that you can pack up and go somewhere else.

They are having their rainy season, so I guess it will take more than one day [to film the match]. It starts raining around two p.m. every day. Mason Rudolph plays Gardner Dickinson. The next week we fly to Eleuthera. Palmer plays Boros. At Miami, Gay Brewer plays Billy Casper. So we do have some great matches coming this year. In Washington Snead plays DeVicenzo.

Ever since we left N.Y. we have been to one cocktail party after another. Jimmy said they should change the name of the show to *Shell's Wonderful World of Parties.* If this doesn't kill you nothing will. But he sure enjoys them. After two drinks he starts singing. I have learned the disappearing act.

This is the first time in six years that I am really enjoying the trip. I am traveling very light. And the work is becoming fun. I haven't seen the course but they have a cart for us so that's not too bad. Cheerio, Gene.

From Penina Golf Hotel, Portimao, Portugal, May 22, 1967

Dear Bob

Here I am down in the tip of Portugal. It's a beautiful place. The climate is perfect. The course was designed by Henry Cotton. I haven't played it yet. Jimmy said it was terrible. But then I don't go by what he thinks, because these Texans can't see anything but Texas.

This is our sixth show [i.e., season on the air]. So we are riding the waves pretty well. The last match in Washington was not too good. I never did see Snead hit the ball so badly. Even nine iron shots were pushed off into traps. Robert De played well, but putted terribly. The season was far behind and the grass on the greens was poor. All in all, the only thing that will look good is Washington and all its beautiful flowers.

This course [Penina] was laid out in rice paddies. I never realized that Portugal was such a great rice producing country. But I can't understand why they would pick out a site like this, miles from the ocean beaches, to build a beautiful hotel when the outlying country is high and rolling, full of beautiful trees, etc. The golf course is on a flat piece of land. I welcome that, easy walking. No golf carts here. We will all use the shoemaker's cart.

Our next stop is St. Andrews, Scotland. If my memory serves me right, the food at the Rusack Hotel is terrible. The weather is undependable. So I'll stay down here. This is a beautiful hotel with excellent food, and good water, which blends in well with Old Rarity.

From the Rusack Hotel, St. Andrews, Scotland, May 27, 1967

Dear Bob

This is just a reminder, and to bring back memories of yesteryear.

Arrived from Portugal. Left some beautiful weather for fog and rain. But then, this place wouldn't look natural if it didn't blow and rain. It's green. Jimmy didn't think much of the place. But I keep telling him this is original and the cradle of golf and I hope they never make a change. These Texans are something.

The people are so nice. They show in their expression how glad they are to see you. I hope the weather is kind to us so we can give it our best. I have a beautiful room, 228, overlooking the 18th fairway. I could almost see Hell's Bunker at a distance, and my mind turns back 34 years ago when I took an eight on that 14th hole to lose the title by one stroke. Thousands of people are roaming the course. It's Sunday, and the Old Course is closed.

I hope you enjoy these short notes as much as I enjoy sitting down and reliving some of the past, when you and I were young. O Boy. Cheerio, Gene.

From Germantown, NY, July 8, 1967

Dear Bob

Here I am back on the farm. It's like being in heaven. The trip is getting harder every year for the old man.

We have some very good shows for you this coming winter. It's all according to the boys that do the cutting. That Jimmy is a long-winded talker. They will have to cut his talk down a lot.

The place I enjoyed most this year was Lausanne, Switzerland. Beau Rivage Hotel. I think that I wrote you about our show in Portugal. I just can't imagine a player like Cotton without any imagination. Terrible course. Cheerio, Gene.

From Marco Island, Florida, Nov. 12, 1967

Dear Bob

We arrived here several days ago to take up our new winter residence. We purchased an apartment on this beautiful beach. How can you beat it. Golf, fishing, and swimming. The climate here is much warmer than Bellair. The 1968 shows are being edited. We go on in late January. We have some great matches. Palmer and Boros, a hole in one in Spain. This is our best year.

From Marco Island, Florida, Dec. 4, 1967

Dear Bob

It was nice hearing from you. Life is beautiful at this tropical island. I feel sorry for those people living up north. I just received my set of irons and woods. In the new aluminum shafts. That's the end of the steel era for golf clubs. I expect to be in Atlanta on Jan. 16th for one of those hectic press parties. I will call you. Maybe we can sit down for a visit. My best to you, Gene.

From Germantown, NY, Jan. 20, 1968

Dear Bob

It was nice spending a half hour with you, but felt terrible to interfere with your lunch. I arrived at the studio just in time for the TV interview. We had a very nice party, had a few Old Rarity, fired the old bull, and went on to Toronto the next morning.

I have never seen so much snow and ice as I saw at the airport in Toronto. My heart bleeds for people who have to live in a cold country like Canada. Marco [Island] is just too beautiful to describe. My Mary is playing golf every day, which I know will make her feel better. If she could only stop smoking so many cigarettes.

I enclosed a rough sketch of the fifth hole [at Augusta National]. I firmly believe this shallow flash trap would make the hole harder for the man who pushes his drive to the right. It also brings the left side into play. The trap should be at least 10 feet from the green. But it should be visible from the right side, not blind. I know the pros would complain about it, but then that means it's a good trap.

I am going to Washington for a showing at the Burning Tree Club of the Palmer-Boros match. If you want me to I'll be glad to stop off at Augusta and look the fifth hole over and stake the trap out.

As I told you during my visit, I am not traveling with the show this coming year. I have had seven wonderful years without a mishap. Jimmy has decided he will go. They are changing the format this year. So complicated that I don't even know myself how it goes. More power to the Madison Avenue boys. As you know, Gordon Biggar is retired and the new crowd wants a change. Best, Gene.

From Germantown, NY, April 15, 1969

Dear Bob

My trip to Augusta was not complete. I had hopes of seeing you at the dinner. But Bob Jr. told me you were not up to it. I was sorry. We missed you.

I played two rounds, but I am afraid my golfing days are over. I have a very bad right shoulder. I finished three out of the last five holes in seven over par.

From all appearances the Masters was about the greatest ever. At least it looked it on TV. Great show. The golf course was in fine shape, and the greens were perfect. Very fast and firm. The whole place looked just too beautiful. Flowers in full bloom, the gallery was very well controlled, and on their best behavior. I want to tell you the galleries today spend more time on their dressing apparel than ever. Long hair with sideburns, but very inspiring to see the miniskirts. It's show business at its best. My very best to you both, Gene.

From Miyako Hotel, Kyoto, Japan, Feb. 8, 1970

Dear Bob

I came through Atlanta very early last week en route to Tokyo. Too early to call [you]. Arrived here last Tuesday. Cold as hell. Will be glad to get back to Mary.

This country has gone into a complete transformation since my last visit four years ago. New hotels, highways, railways, suburbs. It looks very prosperous. New skyscrapers everywhere. Why shouldn't they? No defense spending. Uncle Sam picks up all the bills.

Yesterday I played at the Kyoto Golf Club. They have two courses, 2,500 members. The ground was frozen and I had two sweaters on, and the Japanese were playing in their shirtsleeves. Golf is growing everywhere. But they are running out of land. Big driving nets all over the place. Driving ranges two and three stories high. Hundreds of pleasure-seeking golfers, open all nite. These people are nuts.

In the next five years you are going to hear from this crowd. They have the money now, and are ready to make their mark. I have one more week's work, then on to Honolulu to thaw out.

I was somewhat disappointed in the Shell shows this year. That three-man format was not my doing. The live tournaments are putting on a good show. I don't mean tour events like Crosby, Hope, and Andy Williams. I mean the big events.

Cheerio, Gene.

From Marco Island, Florida, April 14, 1970

Dear Bob

I had hopes of seeing you at the Masters, but was informed by Cliff [Roberts] that the trip was more than you could take.

The Masters [Champions] dinner was very quiet. Hogan came, and left the next morning. The weather was beautiful throughout. You would have loved the greens, just perfect. The fairways showed signs of a hard winter. It was by far the greatest tournament ever. We keep saying this every year.

I practiced very hard for this year's tournament, but got off to a very bad start taking a seven on number two. My ball buried in a tree, and I had to take a two stroke penalty. My walking on the beach at Marco Island sure paid off. I wasn't tired. Now I must take off a few pounds.

My next big event will be the British Open. I'll think of you when walking down those rugged fairways [at Troon].

We are all finished with the Shell shows. They have decided nine years was enough. Well Bob, the years are going by too damn fast. It was 50 years ago when I first saw you at Toledo.

The farm is up for sale. I have Florida as my home now. But not year-round. When the farm sells I'll get a summer home in New Hampshire.

My Mary has fallen in love with golf again, playing four days a week. Gene Jr. has moved down to Boca Raton, works for IBM. He loves Florida, has two children. My daughter has four children, and lives in Newtonville, Mass.

I saw Bob Jr. and family at the Masters. They all looked well. I had promised to go over for a drink, but it's an empty cottage without you and Mary there.

My very best to both of you. Gene.

Twenty months after Gene Sarazen's last letter from the road to his old and dear friend, Bob Jones died at the age of 69.